SMASHING PLATES

Maria Elia

Maria Elia

SMASHING PLATES

Greek Flavors Redefined

Photography by Jenny Zarins

Kyle Books

Published in 2014 by Kyle Books
www.kylebooks.com
general.enquiries@kylebooks.com

Distributed by National Book Network
4501 Forbes Blvd., Suite 200
Lanham, MD 20706
Phone: (800) 462-6420
Fax: (800) 338-4550
customercare@nbnbooks.com

ISBN: 978-1-909487-06-2

10 9 8 7 6 5 4 3 2 1

Maria Elia is hereby identified as the author of this work in
accordance with section 77 of Copyright, Designs and Patents
Act 1988.

Photography: Jenny Zarins
Design: BuroCreative
Prop styling: Tabitha Hawkins
Food styling: Linda Tubby & Maria Elia
Project editor: Sophie Allen
Copy editor: Emily Hatchwell
Editorial assistant: Tara O'Sullivan
Photographer's assistant: Georgie Clarke
Production: Nic Jones and David Hearn

Library of Congress Control Number: 2013956794

Color reproduction by ALTA London
Printed and bound in China by C & C Offset Printing Co. Ltd.

The love of sharing good food is an integral part of Greek culture and one that is central to my earliest childhood memories.

I was nine years old the first time I visited Cyprus. I remember the drive to the Troodos Mountains high up in the sky—scary narrow dirt roads with no barriers; my mother, petrified, shouting at my dad not to go so close to the edge! We arrived in Gerakis, the village where my dad grew up (a far cry from our London life). He showed us his beloved island and I finally met ALL my relatives, including my Pappoo (my grandfather) for the first time. I remember picking almonds and walnuts with my cousins; it had never occurred to me up until then that they grew on trees! The whole trip, especially the food, left a lasting impression, and added to the passion I'd already developed for Greek food.

I knew from the age of four that I wanted to be a chef, and my earliest memories are of sharing food with my family. I was raised in the restaurant owned by my Greek Cypriot father and English mother. The buzz, excitement, and aromas of the kitchen had me spellbound—it was the place I was happiest and where my palate first developed a love of Greek flavors. Sundays were frequently spent at "another" Greek wedding (hence the inspiration behind the book title) or at my Aunty Stella's house. She always prepared a banquet of Greek delicacies; it was food that made my taste buds come alive.

On the rare occasions my dad cooked for us at home, I'd be so excited! He'd often make a pork dish that I loved so much, I can taste it as I write now. Tender cubes of pork cooked with sticky caramelized onions, served with a tomato rice pilaf—creamy with olive oil and butter—simply delicious, as were the peas. As a child I'd only ever eaten peas "Greek-style," slow-braised in a rich tomato sauce scented with cinnamon and dill. If peas were given to me any other way I would try to hide them under my mashed potatoes. My poor mother—I loved her cooking, but she cooked because we needed to eat; it was never a passion of hers. She's creative in other ways instead; she used to make us the most beautiful clothes!

Family life changed when my dad lost his restaurant and my parents divorced. I didn't see my dad so often after that (he eventually moved back to Cyprus), and I lost touch with the Greek side of my family—and, of course, the food. My mom worked odd shifts and I used to cook for me and my sister after

school, experimenting with whatever was in the fridge or growing in the garden. I loved to read through the Robert Carrier and *Taste* magazines Mom used to buy. But I didn't eat "Greek" for a long while.

After I finished school, I did a five-year apprenticeship, and then embraced my cheffing career, which opened my eyes to a whole wealth of amazing flavors and cuisines.

But in recent years those flavors of Greece, and particularly Cyprus, have come back to me. They are the ones that are most emotive to me; the ones that make my heart sing. So I decided to rediscover them by spending the summer cooking with my Dad at his village taverna in the Troodos mountains. The trip was filled with nostalgia—I'd visited only twice since my first trip, each time taking for granted the stunning beauty of those mountains and rural life. The villagers welcomed me into their homes, taught me new and old recipes, shared produce from their gardens, and even tried to teach me Greek! I went hunting with my dad and gathered caper leaves for pickling.

I went to Cyprus to embrace my love of Greek food, but what I also discovered was an abundance of inspiring ingredients that I was now seeing through the eyes of an adult chef; ingredients I could take on a new culinary journey. The recipes in this book do just that—they redefine the Greek ingredients that I love, with my own contemporary twist. There's nothing more I'd like than to see Greek cuisine elevated to the level it so deserves, away from the greasy moussakas and doner kebabs it is so often associated with!

If you love the fresh flavors of Greece and its islands as I do, these recipes will transport you back there, to memories shared and experienced, through nothing more than a simple plate of food. I hope the recipes in this book give you new insight into Greek cuisine. And I hope they bring much happiness to you and whoever you choose to share them with.

USING THIS BOOK

The recipes in this book have been inspired in one way or another by the food of my Greek heritage and my travels through Greece, its islands, and Cyprus, and by the people who generously shared their love of Greek food with me through their stories and food, welcoming me into their homes with their ever-generous Greek hospitality.

Greek meal times consist of an abundance of food that adorns the table; it's food that is always shared rather than individually plated. The recipes in this book are structured into four sections. Most have been designed for sharing and can be mixed and matched to create a modern Greek meal to share among your friends and family, where plates of food are placed on the table for guests to help themselves.

Mix and match whatever seasonal recipes you'd like with a couple of recipes from small plates, two or three from sides to include a grain and salad, and also a main dish, followed by something sweet. For example: Carrot Keftedes (page 18), Carrot Tabbouleh (page 149), Pomegranate Skordalia (page 131), Slow-roasted Paper-wrapped Leg of Lamb (page 105), Sumac Flatbread (page 159), and Lemon and Dill Braised Fava beans (page 135), followed by Commandaria, Chocolate, and Fig Trifle (page 178). (All invites for the above meal are gladly accepted and can be sent to my email address; I'll be there in a flash!)

For something lighter, try some of the smaller plates with some of the side dishes. For example: Greek Spiced Chicken Livers (page 60), Honeyed Fried Feta (page 29), White Bean, Artichoke, and Basil Hummus (page 136) with crudités, Olive, Caper, and Herb Stuffed Sardines (page 48), and some crusty bread.

Alternatively, go with a rustic family-style sharing dish, such as Wild Greens Macaroni and Cheese (page 69); or something more elaborate like a plated meal consisting of Beet, Apple, and Feta Curd (page 26) for starters, Rabbit Baklava (page 93) for a main dish, and, if you really want to push the envelope for dessert, "Greek Coffee on a Plate" (pages 172–177).

A quick note for vegetarians:

If you're vegetarian, there's plenty for you, too, such as Kalamata Olive Gnocchi (page 83), and some of the main courses can be adapted—for example, the Dried Fig Leaf Pasta Rags with Serrano Ham, Figs, and Cheese (page 118) can be made without the ham, without compromising on flavor. Many of the side dishes are dishes in their own right, so I am sure you will feel there's enough choice for you.

Cheese is a very useful, protein-rich alternative to meat, but it's important to note that a lot of cheeses contain animal ingredients, such as rennet, and are therefore not strictly suitable for a vegetarian diet. The good news is that not all cheeses are made with this product as there is a type of rennet that is derived from plants and bacteria. So you can buy vegetarian halloumi, feta, or Parmesan (to use instead of Kefalotyri)—just look for a vegetarian symbol on the label.

A few tips for whatever you choose to cook:

Choose recipes with ingredients that are in season— not only will they taste a hundred times better, they'll also be cheaper and readily available, and you should be able to buy them locally.

Choose recipes that use cooking methods you have space for. Balance the recipes out between what kitchen equipment you have, i.e., between the stove, oven, broiler, and grill, etc.

Think about cooking dishes to create a balance of those served hot, cold, and at room temperature.

When entertaining, think about which recipes you can prepare in advance, so that you just need to make the finishing touches and you actually get to enjoy your guests' company rather than slaving away in the kitchen alone! A lot of the dishes in this book actually benefit from being cooked a day ahead, allowing the flavors to develop.

THE GREEK PANTRY

The basis of good Greek cooking is already there, waiting for you in the cupboard.

Greek cuisine is based on ingredients rather than techniques, encompassing the seasonality (which is celebrated) and freshness of ingredients. It's all about taking the simplest ingredients and turning them into delicious, flavorful dishes, preserving their natural textures and tastes. The Mediterranean climate and nutrient-rich soil provide an exciting abundance of fresh ingredients.

Here are just a few key basic ingredients that are essential for your Smashing Plates *pantry:*

If you happen to live in a big city, you can probably find some great quality Greek, Middle Eastern or Turkish supermarkets that stock many of the ingredients listed, as do many other supermarkets. Alternatively, there are a number of online retailers specializing in authentic Greek and Mediterranean produce (page 15).

OLIVE OIL
Greece is one of the largest producers of olive oil in the world, and it is the life blood of Greek cuisine. Look for "new season" olive oil, which is deliciously pungent, fruity, and bright green in color—Iliada is a favorite of mine. Use extra-virgin olive oil for finishing dishes and olive oil to cook with. Olive oil is drizzled over practically everything and used in anything from salad dressings, soups, and skordalia to cakes. It's the fuel that keeps the flame alight beneath the icons of patron saints in small walled village shrines and is used to mark the sign of the cross at a child's baptism.

OLIVES
There are dozens of varieties of olives to choose from, some named by provenance, others by type, Kalamata being one of the most famous. They are plump and fleshy and green, purple, or black depending on their state of ripeness when harvested. Not only an essential part of any mezze, they add salty richness to bread, stews, salads, and sauces.

CAPERS
These plants grow wild throughout Greece and the Greeks love to use the tender stems and leaves as much as the buds, which they pickle in brine or vinegar or preserve in salt (see Dino's Pickled Caper Leaves on page 153). Capers add a lovely salty sharpness and acidity to a dish—they're particularly addictive when fried until crisp.

GARLIC
Garlic is one of the foundations of Greek cooking. It appears in virtually every savory recipe, with skordalia being the famous garlic sauce.

HERBS
Oregano, or Rigani: The quintessential Greek herb that grows wild all over Greece and its islands. The Greeks often use the dried flower buds of the plant rather than the leaves. An essential herb for everyday use, delicious in marinades, sprinkled over grilled meats, fish, and the classic village (Greek) salad, or made into a fragrant salt with dried lemon zest. Rigani is stronger and sharper than regular oregano, so use in smaller quantities.

Dill: Like oregano, dill grows across the whole of Greece. One of the most versatile of herbs, delicate and aromatic, it is essential for tzatziki and fabulous with peas, lamb, potatoes, and greens. Use fresh wherever possible.

Mint: There are many varieties that grow wild across Greece, often used in combination with dill, oregano, and parsley. Dried is as fragrant as fresh. Use it sparingly in meat, yogurt, and cheese dishes, and add a sprinkle to feta curd.

Parsley: Since antiquity, parsley is the most widely used herb in Greek cooking. It makes its way into almost everything, adding an abundance of freshness. The Greeks only use flat-leaf parsley.

Bay: Not only are bay leaves used to flavor sweet and savory dishes, they were also woven into honorary wreaths for triumphant Olympians, warriors, and poets!

SPICES

Anise: Indigenous to the Greek islands, anise is an essential ingredient in Greek cuisine, used to flavor everything from ouzo to cakes, bread, and fish dishes. Buy in small quantities as it quickly loses its flavor. (Star anise is the Asian equivalent, which is stronger in taste, so use more sparingly if substituting.)

Cinnamon: One of my absolute favorites, its sweet spicy fragrance fills the air with childhood memories. A spice that is present in just about anything from sweet to savory dishes, adding depth and earthiness.

Fennel seed: Another one of my all-time favorite ingredients, sweet and anise-flavored fennel seed adds freshness and life to any dish from pork and fish to bread and sweet dishes, and is exceptionally great when ground with sugar to dust doughnuts (page 176). Dry-roasting the seed will intensify the flavor. Don't miss the opportunity to use wild fennel in the summer; its flavor is sensational. Interesting fact: in Ancient Greece, a wreath of fennel was a symbol of success.

Allspice, cloves, coriander, cumin, and nutmeg are also sprinkled throughout the book.

SESAME SEEDS

These have been used to flavor breads since antiquity, often with poppy, flax, anise, cumin, and caraway seeds, and they form the base of tahini.

TAHINI

Tahini is an oil-based paste made from roasted sesame seeds. An essential ingredient in hummus, it's also used as the base for a great flavored simple sauce with or without the addition of yogurt; it's delicious with chocolate in desserts and peanuts in ice cream. Mix the liquid part that sits at the top of the jar with the rest of the paste. Tahini varies in quality, and is best purchased from a Greek or Middle Eastern store. Ask the other customers which one they think is best!

BEANS AND GRAINS

Black-eyed peas, fava beans, yellow split peas, lentils, and chickpeas are just a few of the essential legumes that make up the Greek pantry. So significant are beans to Greek cuisine the Gigantes even have their own PDO (Protected Designation of Origin), as do the yellow split peas of Santorini. The quality of dried beans can differ dramatically, so always try and buy the best quality available. Beans that are old will take much longer to cook and their skins are usually tough. Grains also play a significant part in the Greek diet and include barley, pourgouri (bulgur wheat), rice, and orzo (which is in fact not a grain but a small type of pasta).

DRIED FRUIT

Raisins and currants are used in sweet and savory dishes, adding a sweet and almost sour element. They're particularly good with fish and tomato dishes. Try presoaking them in Commandaria wine or Metaxa brandy for an extra flavor hit. Dates are another favorite ingredient. If you can't find fresh Greek dates, substitute with Medjool; they add a caramelized sweetness and depth of texture to any dish.

NUTS

An essential delicacy in Greek cuisine, and always served as an accompaniment to beer!

Almonds: Almonds have been the Greeks' favorite nut since 10,000 BC! They are used with garlic to make skordalia, and in pastries with honey. Symbolic at Greek weddings, sugar-coated almonds are given to guests, presented in odd numbers in little mesh bags tied with white ribbon. Loukoumia (a most delicious sugar-dusted almond cookie) are also given, and they were one of the things I looked forward to most when dragged to a wedding every Sunday as a kid. I'd pretty much put almonds in everything if I could. The "skin-on" varieties are so much tastier than blanched and nothing beats a freshly shelled almond off the tree. Cyprus is famous for its Soutzoukos, a chewy sweet made by dipping strings of almonds into a kind of grape jelly.

Walnuts: One of my first memories of Cyprus is shelling fresh walnuts with my cousins and having walnut-stained hands. They are often used in baklava, cakes, or preserved as a spoon sweet in a thick sugar syrup (page 52). I like to serve them with grapes and partridge—three ingredients that are not only seasonally harmonious (the ethos behind most of my dishes), but also taste delicious together.

Pistachios: Pistachios are harvested in August or September. The red fruit is left to dry in the sun for 24 hours before being muddled in water to separate the nut from its flesh, which is then dried again before being processed, either naturally or roasted.

CHEESES

Here are just three of the vast number of stunning cheeses produced by the Greeks:

Feta: Another quintessential ingredient and one of the most famous of Greek cheeses, traditionally made from 70 percent sheep's and 30 percent goat's milk. Feta is left to ripen in barrels or jugs filled with brine for three months—barrel-matured feta is the tastiest. Creamy and pungent, salty and sour, it can be used in so many ways, adding a depth of flavor and texture to almost any dish. One of Greece's many cheeses with Protected Designation of Origin (PDO), feta means "slice."

Kefalotyri: A hard and salty cheese made from a blend of sheep's and goat's milk. It's pale yellow in color and literally translates as "head" cheese, named after its shape. It's great for grating over pasta or stifado dishes. The nearest substitute is Pecorino or Parmesan.

Halloumi: Cyprus's most famous cheese. Traditionally made with goat's milk, although nowadays often made with a mixture of sheep's and sometimes a little cow's milk, much to the disgust of the Cypriots. Rich and salty and flavored with dried mint, I urge you to try making it yourself (see page 34) or try some fresh halloumi whenever possible—there really is a massive difference between the fresh version and the commercial, vacuum-packed "squeaky" variety sold in the supermarkets.

HONEY

Greek honey is one of the most highly prized honeys in the world. The rich flora of Greece and its islands provides a paradise for bees to feed on. From fragrant orange blossom in the spring, to flowering thyme and pine in the summer to heather and chestnut in the winter. If I were a bee I'd want to be Greek! (The Greek word for honey is "Mele" and "Melissa" means honey bee.) More than just a food, honey is known for its medicinal properties and has also played a role in Greek mythology. Fir honey from Vitina in the Peloponnese has its very own PDO. Look out for the Attiki brand, a rich, aromatic honey produced from bees that collect nectar from Greek thyme and wild flowers. It's utterly delicious!

TOMATO PASTE

An essential ingredient to Greek cuisine, Greek tomato paste is particularly special as it's made from small, sweet Greek tomatoes and has a deeply rich, concentrated taste.

YOGURT

Made from either sheep's, goat's, or cow's milk, Greek yogurt is renowned the world over for its thick, dreamy cream texture and sour flavor. Often sold as a strained yogurt, you can make your own by placing yogurt in a strainer lined with cheesecloth over a bowl. Place a weight on the top and leave for several hours in the fridge. Use as a substitute for sour cream or roll into balls around walnuts or almonds, drizzle with honey, and roll in chopped mint for a tasty snack!

VINEGAR

An indispensable ingredient in any Greek kitchen, vinegar adds life to a dish, from salads to sauces to stews (stifados). Vinegars vary dramatically in quality; I like to stock a variety, as a good-quality vinegar will make such a difference to a finished dish. If you can't find Greek-aged wine vinegars, look for the Spanish brand Forum—Cabernet Sauvignon and Chardonnay are particular favorites of mine.

ROSE WATER

Roses—the flowers of love—are associated with the goddess Aphrodite. Rose petals are harvested in May and distilled into rose oil and water. Some rose waters contain extract of rose essence (the oil) so it's best to use them sparingly as their flavor is so concentrated. Rose water adds a wonderful delicate floral bouquet and aroma to many sweet and savory dishes. You'll find the quality of rose water really does vary; again, I'd recommend buying from a Greek or Middle Eastern supplier. One tablespoon of rose water is equal to about 1 teaspoon of rose essence.

ORANGE FLOWER WATER

Like rose water, orange flower water is distilled from the gorgeously fragrant blossoms of the orange tree. It's a fragrance I love and one that can delicately transform a dish, sweet or savory. Again, use sparingly. The golden rule for both flower waters is: you can always add more, but you can't take away.

LEMONS

Lemons are one of the most basic and important elements of Greek cuisine, adding flavor to almost every dish. Not necessarily a pantry ingredient, but one you would be lost without.

OUZO

Ouzo is an anise-flavored aperitif, distilled from raisins, figs, grapes, or various sugar sources. It's diluted with water and flavored according to each producer's secret recipe with herbs, citrus, and anise, including flavors such as fennel seed, star anise, cardamom, and coriander. In Lesbos they even add a little mastic. It's left to infuse overnight before being distilled twice in vast copper vats. There are some exceptional ouzos such as Ouzo Babatzim, which undergoes three distillations, the last being over an olive wood fire, to produce the highest quality ouzo. It's also the inspiration for my stuffed slow-roasted rabbit dish (page 94), which combines the elements of herbs and flavors used in ouzo production before being cooked over olive wood. Ouzo personifies the Greek way of life, served neat in a glass or accompanied by a small glass of ice and one of water, which when added makes the drink cloudy. Ouzo has an alcohol content of around 40 percent and its high sugar content delays the release of alcohol, so watch out! Not only is ouzo a refreshing aperitif to enjoy with mezze, it's also wonderful as an ingredient, adding a little "sophistication" and depth of flavor to a dish. It's particularly great with fish dishes and the Greeks like to use it to flavor snails; it's often used in desserts and pastries too. In Greece you can enjoy an ouzo at an ouzeria where you can sample a wide range of regionally produced varieties. Suitable alternatives include sambuca, pastis, or raki.

METAXA

Greece's legendary brandy has a unique and delicious taste produced by a double distillation of wine made from sun-dried grapes. The brandy is then matured in oak barrels for a number of years. It contains a secret blend of Greek herbs, spices, and rose petals, and is blended with aged Muscat wine from Limnos and Samos, then left to further mature in oak barrels. The distinctive Metaxa stars on the bottle indicate the number of years it's matured for, 3 being the minimum, 25 being the "Private Reserve," which never leaves Greece! Enjoy Metaxa on the rocks, with a coffee, or combined with chocolate, raisins, and nuts for a decadent dessert.

COMMANDARIA

Commandaria is a deliciously honey-sweet and spiced dessert wine from Cyprus (see page 178 for more information).

MAVRODAPHNE

Mavrodaphne is a delicious port-like wine made in Patras in the Peloponnese. Deep red in color, cherry-rich and raisin-like in taste and matured in oak barrels for at least two years, it's a stunning wine that goes well with "Greek Coffee on a Plate" (page 172), Plum and Lavender Baklava (page 200), and blue cheese. It's also served at Holy Communion! Substitute with port if unavailable, although some gourmet supermarkets do stock it.

RETSINA

The wine most commonly associated with Greece, and one which you'll either love or hate thanks to its distinctive taste of pine resin! A small amount of Aleppo pine is added to the barrels of fermenting wine, one of the best being Kourtaki's retsina of Attica. Its fragrant taste is best enjoyed over a lazy taverna lunch with plates of fresh fried sardines, barbecued lamb cutlets, feta, and a salad or two on a balmy summer's day... ah, bliss! Alternatively, serve with—and add a glug to—my recipe for a Greek-style Paella (page 84).

GREEK WINES

I could ramble on for pages about my love of Greek wines. My one urge is that you don't base your judgement of Greek wine entirely on retsina. Greece and its islands have the most perfect conditions for viticulture and produce a wide range of fabulous grape varieties. Winemakers have turned their backs on traditional methods of vinification and are blending their grapes using New World and French methods to produce some stunning results. In a blind tasting recently a wine connoisseur friend of mine was shocked to discover that what he thought was a Pulignay Montrachet was in fact a wine from Greece. Some of Santorini's flinty wines are giving Chablis a run for its money. Greek wine is definitely on the up and its recognition is continually growing.

GREEK COFFEE

Part of the staple Greek diet and one of the most important ingredients in a Greek pantry. See page 171 for all you need to know.

GREEK FOOD AND WINE SUPPLIERS

Christos Marketplace
Arlington, MA
www.christosmarket.com

Greek International Food Market
West Roxbury, MA
www.greekintlmarket.com

iGourmet
www.igourmet.com

Parthenon Foods
Milwaukee, WI
www.parthenonfoods.com

Titan Foods
New York, NY
www.titanfoods.net

Wine Chateau
www.winechateau.com

¹/ SMALL PLATES

CARROT KEFTEDES

Normally, keftedes are made with ground meat (they're basically meatballs). These vegetarian alternatives are packed with flavor. Pre-roasting the carrots brings out their natural sweetness which is balanced by the salty, sour feta and Kefalotyri. Mint and parsley add freshness, with a hint of cinnamon for spice. Serve with Pomegranate Skordalia and Carrot Tabbouleh on pages 131 and 149. These keftedes are just as delicous served cold.

Serves 4 (makes 16)

12oz carrots, trimmed and peeled but left whole
2 tablespoons olive oil
1 small onion, grated
1 cup feta, crumbled
½ cup fresh bread crumbs
1 teaspoon cinnamon
2 teaspoons dried mint
½ cup grated Parmesan or Kefalotyri
¼ cup finely chopped fresh flat-leaf parsley
1 free-range egg, beaten
sea salt and freshly ground black pepper
all-purpose flour, to dust
olive or vegetable oil, for frying

Preheat the oven to 400°F.

Place the carrots in a roasting pan. Drizzle with the olive oil and cook for 30–40 minutes (depending on the size of carrots) until al dente, turning them halfway through. Let cool.

Grate the carrots into a bowl and mix with the rest of the ingredients, except the flour and oil. Season with salt and pepper and refrigerate for an hour to firm up. (The mixture can be made the day before and refrigerated until required.)

Shape into 16 walnut-sized balls, then flatten into patties and dust with flour. You can either shallow-fry them in olive oil or deep-fry them in vegetable oil. If using olive oil, heat in a frying pan over medium heat, add half the keftedes, and cook until golden on either side—about 3 minutes. Repeat with the remaining balls. If using vegetable oil, deep-fry for about 3 minutes at 350°F until golden. Drain on paper towels and serve warm with the suggested accompaniments.

GIGANTES PLAKI

I think gigantes plaki is one of the dishes I most look forward to when visiting Greece. Gigantes are "giant beans" and they're well worth tracking down for their exceptional meaty texture, which absorbs flavors like a sponge. "Plaki-style" means cooked in a flat dish or skillet. Personally, I think these beans are best made the day before as this allows the flavors to infuse. Serve them warm or at room temperature, drizzled with olive oil and an optional splash of red wine vinegar. They're also great on toast (see opposite).

Serves 6

1lb dried gigantes
  (if unavailable, substitute with dried butter beans)
½ cup olive oil
1 Spanish onion, finely chopped
1 celery rib, finely chopped (with the leaves, if you have them)
3 garlic cloves, finely chopped
1 tablespoon tomato paste
1 tablespoon finely chopped fresh oregano or 1 teaspoon dried
1lb 2oz vine-ripened plum tomatoes, peeled and
  roughly chopped
1 bay leaf
1 teaspoon sugar
sea salt and freshly ground black pepper
¼ cup finely chopped fresh flat-leaf parsley

Soak the beans overnight in plenty of cold water. Drain, rinse, and place in a large saucepan. Cover with plenty of cold water and bring to a boil. Reduce the heat and simmer until just tender, about 50 minutes. Drain the beans, reserving the cooking liquid, and set both aside.

Preheat the oven to 325°F.

Heat the olive oil in a saucepan and add the onion, celery, and garlic. Cook over medium heat until softened. Add the tomato paste and cook for another minute before adding the oregano, tomatoes, bay leaf, and sugar, along with the beans and 2½ cups of the reserved liquid. Season with salt and pepper and heat.

Pour into a large roasting pan, cover with foil, and place in the oven for about 1–1½ hours, until the beans are tender (the time will depend on the age of the beans); if the beans look a little dry, add a dash of boiling water. Remove the foil and cook for another 30 minutes, uncovered, until most of the liquid has been absorbed and the beans are very tender.

Season to taste and cool a little before adding the parsley. Serve warm or at room temperature.

GIGANTES PLAKI ON TOAST WITH CHERRY TOMATOES, FETA, AND MINT

This is fabulous for brunch, served topped with a poached egg or some sliced loukaniko (pork and lamb sausage) for a cowboy breakfast!

Serves 4

½ of the Gigantes Plaki, see left
⅔ cup cherry tomatoes, halved
4 slices of olive bread, sourdough,
  or ciabatta
a good glug of extra-virgin olive oil
2 tablespoons shredded fresh mint leaves
1 cup feta, crumbled (or other cheese of
  your choice, shaved or grated)

Gently warm the gigantes with the cherry tomatoes over low heat. Preheat a grill pan, drizzle the bread on either side with olive oil, and toast until lightly browned on either side. Stir the mint through the beans and spoon over the toasted bread. Top with cheese and a drizzle of oil and serve.

CAULIFLOWER SOUP WITH FAVA BEANS, FETA, ALMONDS, MINT, AND LEMON

I like to use a little candied lemon peel (see opposite) to garnish this soup, but you can use freshly grated lemon zest instead. It's also great served with some sliced loukaniko, a Greek semi-dried pork sausage flavored with fennel and orange, or you could try it with merguez or chorizo. Crab would work well as a great alternative too… aren't variations the best part of cooking? That's why it takes me forever to write a book: I just go off on tangents—I can't help myself!

Serves 4–6

8oz fresh fava beans, shelled, or 3oz frozen
a glug of olive oil
2 tablespoons butter
2 shallots, finely sliced
1 garlic clove, finely chopped
1 medium cauliflower
3 cups chicken or vegetable stock
¾ cup heavy cream
½ cup slivered almonds
sea salt and freshly ground black pepper

To serve:
½ cup feta, crumbled
8 mint leaves, shredded
candied lemon peel or finely grated zest of ½ lemon
loukaniko sausage (optional)
candied lemon juice (see right) or olive oil

Bring a saucepan of salted water to a boil. Add the fava beans and cook until tender, then refresh under cold running water, drain, peel, and set aside.

Heat a little olive oil and the butter in a pan, add the shallots and garlic, and cook over low heat until softened. Cut the cauliflower into small florets and add to the shallots along with the stock. Bring to a boil and simmer until the cauliflower is tender (about 20 minutes), then add the cream.

While the soup is cooking, prepare the almonds. Heat about 2 tablespoons of olive oil in a frying pan over medium heat, add the almonds, and cook until golden. Drain on paper towels and set aside.

Pour the soup into a blender and process until smooth. Pour into a clean pan and place over the heat. Season with salt and pepper and serve hot, sprinkled with the fava beans, almonds, feta, mint, and a little candied lemon or lemon zest—and slices of sausage, if using. Top with a drizzle of candied lemon juice or olive oil.

CANDIED LEMON PEEL

An instant alternative to preserved lemons. Make a batch and add to tabbouleh, risottos, and tzatziki, or serve with the Pickled Chicken on page 54.

2 organic lemons
½ cup superfine sugar
½ cup water
1 tablespoon white wine vinegar

Remove the rind from the lemons using a vegetable peeler and cut away any white pith. Roll up the zest and cut lengthwise into fine strips, then blanch in boiling water for 30 seconds; repeat twice more, drain, and set aside. (The blanching helps remove any bitterness, so don't try to skip this stage—the results are worth it.)

Bring the sugar and water to a boil in a small saucepan, stirring to dissolve the sugar. Boil for 4 minutes before adding the lemon zest. Cook for 2 minutes then remove from the heat. Stir in the vinegar and cool. Store in the liquid and refrigerate until required.

TOMATO KEFTEDES

I first tasted these while on vacation in Skiathos at the wonderful Rose's Taverna. The lovely owner shared his recipe with me. Originally they're a speciality of Santorini and are eaten during Lent. There are many versions—mine uses bread crumbs to bind, but traditionally just flour is used. Keftedes can be made with a variety of ingredients including meat and fish.

Serve with Greek yogurt, Skordalia (page 130), or Tahini Sauce (page 160). They'd also be delicious with Taramasalata (page 129) and some grilled sardines. These keftedes also taste great cold in a sandwich with roast lamb.

Serves 4–6

4 vine-ripened plum tomatoes, peeled and finely chopped
2 tablespoons grated onion
2 tablespoons chopped fresh mint
3 tablespoons chopped fresh dill
1 teaspoon sugar
pinch of ground cinnamon
½ cup feta cheese, crumbled
½ cup Parmesan or Kefalotyri, grated
½ cup fresh bread crumbs
sea salt and freshly ground black pepper
2 free-range eggs, beaten
¾ cup all-purpose flour
olive or vegetable oil, for frying

Mix the tomatoes, onion, herbs, sugar, cinnamon, feta, Parmesan, and bread crumbs together and season with salt and pepper. Add enough of the beaten eggs to combine and chill the mixture in the fridge for an hour to allow the mixture to firm up.

Season the flour with salt and pepper. Shape the tomato mixture into walnut-sized balls and coat in the seasoned flour. You can make these ahead of time and refrigerate on a paper-lined baking sheet dusted with flour. It's best to store them uncovered if you do—they will keep well for a day or two.

You can either shallow fry the keftedes in olive oil or deep-fry them in vegetable oil. If using olive oil, heat in a frying pan over medium heat. Add the keftedes in batches of 4–5 and cook until golden on either side—about 3 minutes. Repeat with the remaining keftedes. If using vegetable oil, deep-fry for about 3 minutes at 325°F until golden. Drain on paper towels, sprinkle with salt, and serve.

CHESTNUT, CINNAMON, AND BRANDY SOUP WITH WALNUTS AND DATES

In ancient Greece, the chestnut tree was regarded as the tree of Zeus, and festivals in honor of chestnuts are still held throughout the country—not least in the village of Kastanitsa (on the slopes of Mount Parnonas in the Peleponnese), whose name actually means "chestnut"! Toward the end of October every year, the inhabitants of Kastanistsa make a huge range of sweet and savory chestnut dishes to celebrate the chestnut season. So here's one for the festival! The addition of the date is to bring a little spark to the chestnuts.

Variation: If you prefer a non-vegetarian version, try topping with some crispy smoked bacon crumbles: cook the bacon and set aside before cooking the chestnuts, then mix together.

Serves 4

2 tablespoons unsalted butter
½ onion, finely chopped
1 small carrot, finely chopped
1 celery rib, finely chopped
a pinch of ground cinnamon
2 tablespoons chopped thyme leaves
2½ cups cooked chestnuts (includes ½ cup for the topping)
¼ cup Metaxa brandy or sweet sherry
3¼ cups vegetable stock (or try using porcini stock cubes, which are great!)
sea salt and freshly ground black pepper
2 tablespoons walnut pieces
1 Greek or Medjool date, pitted and finely sliced
2 tablespoons walnut oil or extra-virgin olive oil

Heat 1 tablespoon of the butter in a medium saucepan. Add the onion, carrot, and celery and cook over low heat for about 10–15 minutes, until softened. Add the cinnamon, thyme, and 2 cups chestnuts and cook for 2 minutes. Add the brandy and stock and season with salt and pepper. Bring to a boil, then reduce to a simmer and cook for 30 minutes, stirring occasionally.

While the soup is cooking, make the topping. Heat the rest of the butter in a small frying pan then add the walnuts and remaining chestnuts and cook over high heat for a minute.

Blend the soup in batches until smooth, taste for seasoning, and pour into bowls. Top each bowl with the fried chestnuts and walnuts and the sliced date. Serve drizzled with walnut or olive oil.

BEET, APPLE, AND FETA CURD SALAD

A seasonal salad that brings out the best of these beautifully colored beets. Early beets are combined with sweet and sharp apple, and the feta curd adds a subtle softness to this textural dish that's as pretty as a picture once plated. This is how I would present this dish in my restaurant. It's easy and a joy to assemble—and one of my favorite recipes in this book.

Variations: You could try adding cooked puy lentils, blanched fresh peas, seared slices of lamb or beef, or diced roasted pumpkin to the salad, and scatter with roasted pumpkin seeds rather than hazelnuts. Try replacing the hazelnuts and hazelnut oil with walnuts and walnut oil.

Serves 4–6

For the salad:
5 each of small golden, candy cane, and red beets
1 x 7oz package of feta, crumbled
⅔ cup Greek yogurt
sea salt and freshly ground black pepper
vegetable oil, for deep-frying
1 green apple
1 tablespoon superfine sugar
1 curly endive, or frisée
handful of pea shoots
3 tablespoons roasted hazelnuts, roughly chopped or crushed
1 package of edible viola flowers

For the hazelnut dressing:
7 tablespoons hazelnut oil
3 tablespoons cider vinegar
⅔ cup fresh apple cider, boiled until reduced to ¼ cup, then cooled

Preheat the oven to 400°F. Cut off all but ¾in of the stems from four of each type of beet and wash thoroughly. Wrap each in foil and place in a roasting pan. Cook for 30–40 minutes for small beets or 40–60 minutes for medium until tender. Cool a little before gently slipping off the skins, then cut into wedges.

Meanwhile, make the feta curd. Put the feta in a blender with the yogurt and a pinch of black pepper and pulse until smooth. Then whisk the dressing ingredients together, season, and set aside.

Heat the oil to 350°F in a deep-fryer or deep saucepan. Peel and thinly slice the remaining three beets using a mandolin and set half aside. Deep-fry the remaining slices for 1–2 minutes until crisp, then drain on paper towels. Season and set aside.

Now preheat a large frying pan over high heat. Peel the apple and cut into 8 wedges, removing the core. Toss in the sugar and place in the hot pan. The apple wedges will immediately caramelize. Cook until golden and slightly softened, then set aside.

To assemble, smear some feta curd over each plate (see photo for positioning), then scatter with a little curly endive and top with the apple wedges and roasted beets. Scatter artistically with pea shoots, hazelnuts, and raw beets slices, paying attention to color, and drizzle with dressing. Garnish with the beet chips and viola flowers.

HONEYED FRIED FETA

Sometimes the simple things in life are the best, and what could be simpler or more delicious than warm, salty, sour feta drizzled with sweet honey? Greek thyme honey is a particular favorite of mine. Try serving the feta sprinkled with chopped almonds and some fresh figs, or chopped dates or slices of pear or peach.

Serves 4–6

1¾ cups olive oil
2 x 7oz packages of feta
⅔ cup all-purpose flour
3 free-range eggs, beaten
¼ cup honey
2–4 figs, to serve (optional)

Heat the oil in a small frying pan to about 325°F (which means that a cube of bread will brown in 30 seconds). Cut each block of feta in half or into thirds and dust each piece of feta with flour to cover completely. Dip two pieces into the egg and cook in the hot oil until golden on either side.

Carefully remove the feta and drain on paper towels, then repeat with the remaining pieces. Serve immediately, drizzled with honey, with the figs (if using).

CHILE-ROASTED FETA AND WATERMELON WITH RAISIN OREGANO DRESSING

Roasting the feta gives it a lovely soft texture. Spike with chile, serve hot on top of chilled watermelon, and finish with oregano dressing for a match made in heaven. Bursting with sweet, sour, and spice, the raisin oregano dressing gives a full-on flavor that complements not only feta and watermelon, but scallops and soutzouki perfectly.

Serves 2–4 depending on hunger!

For the Raisin Oregano Dressing (makes about ¾ cup)
⅓ cup raisins
1 garlic clove, crushed
2 small shallots, finely chopped
¼ cup Cabernet Sauvignon vinegar
small pinch dried red pepper flakes
finely grated zest of ¼ orange plus 1 tablespoon
   of juice
¼ cup olive oil
⅓ cup extra virgin olive oil
1½ tablespoons finely chopped oregano
sea salt

1 small watermelon
1 x 7oz package of feta, cut widthwise into
   4 even pieces
olive oil, for drizzling
pinch of dried red pepper flakes
1 small handful of mixed leaves, such as mizuna,
   arugula, and dandelion
1 tablespoon toasted pine nuts
shiso sprouts and micro cilantro,
   to garnish (optional)

To make the dressing, soak the raisins in hot water for about 10 minutes until plump, then drain and place in a blender. Add the remaining dressing ingredients and pulse to form a chunky dressing. Season with a pinch of salt and refrigerate until required.

Slice the top and bottom off the watermelon and stand it upright on a work surface. Remove the skin as you would that of an orange, cutting from top to bottom to reveal the melon flesh. Discard the skin and cut the flesh into ¾in thick slices. Cut each slice into rectangular blocks measuring 4 x 2 x ¾in and put in the fridge until required.

Preheat the oven to 375°F. Cut a medium piece of foil, place the feta on one half, drizzle with oil, and sprinkle with red pepper flakes. Fold the foil over to form a loose parckage. Place on a baking sheet and cook for 8–10 minutes or until the feta has softened.

Place a piece of chilled watermelon in the center of each plate and top each with a few leaves, followed by 2 tablespoons of the oregano dressing and a sprinkling of pine nuts. Place the hot feta on top, garnish with shiso sprouts and micro cilantro, if using, and serve immediately.

Use the leftover watermelon to make a feta, watermelon, and mint salad, or see the recipes for Watermelon Mahalepi (page 190), or Watermelon and Greek Basil Ice Pops (page 188).

Variations: Roast the chile-sprinkled feta on some sliced tomato and serve on toast topped with a poached egg and some torn mint leaves for a great breakfast.

FIG-LEAF WRAPPED FETA

One of the Cypriot villagers asked how I came up with this recipe. To me, it was easy—all the ingredients were there, surrounding and inspiring me. I just saw them with different eyes! The mountains are full of fragrant fig trees. The Greeks go nuts for the figs but never use the leaves. An idea sprung to mind to wrap feta in these fragrant leaves and serve them alongside the figs, whose skins were about to burst with flavor, they were so juicy and ripe. Right beside the fig trees stood an almond tree ripe with nuts. It made perfect sense—all these seasonal ingredients were made for each other.

I cooked this dish in my cousin's uncle Nastouras' wood-fired oven (in his garden of paradise!). He was intrigued by the combination and suggested I drizzled the feta with some of his homemade Epsima (grape honey). It proved to be a gorgeous combination. You could of course use regular honey, which would be equally delicious—and you can use grape leaves if fig leaves are unavailable.

If you don't have the luxury of a wood-fired oven, a regular oven will do!

Serves 4

4 large fresh fig leaves, washed and dried
2 x 7oz packages of feta, cut in half
4 figs, torn
16 whole, skin-on almonds, roughly chopped
¼ cup honey

Preheat the oven to 425°F. Lay the fig leaves, vein-side up, on a work surface and place a piece of feta on top of each. Fold over the leaves to make a neat package. Place on a wire rack on top of a baking sheet if cooking in the oven.

Place in the oven and cook for 5–8 minutes until the feta has begun to soften when squeezed and the leaves are fragrant. Remove from the oven, open up the fig-leaf packages, and top with the figs and almonds. Drizzle with honey and serve immediately in the leaves.

GOAT'S MILK RICOTTA

Making halloumi is quite a laborious task, but making ricotta is much simpler. Anari cheese, a by-product of halloumi, is very similar to ricotta. Greeks eat it for breakfast sprinkled with cinnamon and drizzled with honey and rose water. This is a much easier version for sweet or savory use. Goat's ricotta has a creamier texture than cow's and a mild, sweet flavor. If you prefer an even creamier version, replace 1 cup of the goat's milk with heavy cream!

It's delicious served on toasted bread topped with fresh figs, peaches, or strawberries and drizzled with honey, olive oil, or a little balsamic vinegar. Alternatively, try topping with charcuterie, or spoon over Dried Fig Leaf Pasta Rags (page 116). Or serve with Lemon and Dill Braised Fava beans (page 135). The list is endless!

Makes about 7oz

1 quart goat's milk
½ teaspoon sea salt, plus extra to season
5 tablespoons freshly squeezed lemon juice
1 tablespoon dried mint, optional

Heat the milk and salt in a pan over low heat until it reaches 185°F. Remove the pan from the heat and add the lemon juice, stirring just once. Let sit for 5 minutes. During this time the curds will separate from the whey and rise to the top.

Line a colander with a couple of clean pieces of cheesecloth, leaving enough overhang so you can bring the sides together. Ladle rather than pour the curds and whey into the lined colander placed over a large deep bowl and let drain for around 30 minutes.

Bring the corners of the cloth together and tie, making a loop at the top. Hang the cheese bundle over a bowl or a bucket to catch the drained whey. Let drain for 1–1½ hours, depending on how dense you would like your ricotta to be.

Remove the bundle of cheese and place in a bowl (reserving the whey). Add the dried mint, if using, and season with sea salt. Mix well. Refrigerate for up to 3 days, though it's at its best eaten within 24 hours.

The reserved whey can be used to make Feta Polenta (page 141), the béchamel sauce for the Moussaka-stuffed Tomatoes (page 111), and instead of yogurt in the Banana, Oat, and Almond Smoothie (page 169) or the Bircher Granola (page 168).

Variations: There are lots of things that you can add to the ricotta as flavorings, such as some finely grated lemon or orange rind, or chopped red chile, dried dill, or freshly chopped wild garlic, or a combination of the above. For sweet ricotta add a little superfine sugar, a pinch of cinnamon, and a drop of rose water to taste. Orange flower water also works equally well.

HALLOUMI

While in Cyprus, I had the amazing opportunity to make halloumi with my friend Julia and her family. Julia's daughter-in-law, Vasiliki, heard I was from London and that I was interested in meeting any local villagers who produced their own halloumi, a rarity these days. I arrived in the morning and was greeted by the whole family (all 11 of them!) and a freshly filled 9-gallon churn of unpasteurized goat's milk that they'd collected from their neighbor's farm; these days, it's common to see halloumi made with a mixture of goat's, sheep's and cow's milk rather than the traditional 100 percent goat's. "Ripe" halloumi is often made in Cyprus between April and June, when the goat's or sheep's milk is at its best as a result of them feeding on dry grass, barley, or hay, and the temperature is at an optimum. Thanks to Julia and her family and Mrs. Sophia and her neighbor (that's them in the photo!) for showing me how to make this wonderful cheese. It really was a highlight of my trip to Cyprus.

Before you get started on trying this at home, you'll need some cheesecloth, a colander, a fine mesh sieve, a rubber spatula or wooden spoon, a thermometer, and, most importantly, two halloumi molds—known as talarin. These were originally made of woven rush but now are generally made of plastic; you can buy them online (see page 37). However, I have invented an alternative that you can fashion at home for free: take three plastic pint milk cartons, cut the top third off each, and pierce the bottom part all over, then wash well and line with cheesecloth. Alternatively, a large-holed colander will suffice. Ideally, you'd use raw milk for making the halloumi; otherwise, use whole milk. You'll also need liquid rennet (see page 37).

Halloumi is delicious eaten fresh with some honeydew melon (simply divine: salty, soft cheese with a hint of mint and cold, sweet, juicy melon), or drizzled with a little olive oil and pan-fried, broiled, or grilled with anything you like! Fresh figs, peaches, sardines, olives, strawberries, prosciutto, pears, bitter leaves, tangerines, chiles—all are heavenly accompaniments.

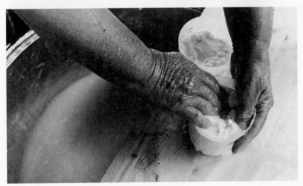

Makes about 1lb 10oz

3 quarts raw goat's, cow's, or sheep's milk (use whole if raw is unavailable)
13 drops liquid vegetarian rennet (the container should have a dropper—see note on page 37)
2 teaspoons white wine vinegar or citric acid (for making Anari)
3 tablespoons sea salt
2 tablespoons dried or chopped fresh mint leaves, to taste

Gently and slowly heat the milk in a large wide pan to 90°F, stirring occasionally. Dissolve the rennet in 2 tablespoons of boiled and cooled water before stirring into the milk.

Cover the pan with a towel to keep it warm, and turn off the heat. Let the milk coagulate (set)—this will take 35–60 minutes. It's important that the temperature stays at 90°F, but a couple of degrees less is fine.

To test if it's ready, place the back of your hand gently on the surface of the milk—it shouldn't stick. Then insert a knife and make a small cut. If the curd forms a "clean break," it's ready. If not, leave a little longer.

Cut the curd with a knife into vertical 1¼in square cubes, then leave to "heal" for 5 minutes before cutting into even-sized horizontal squares.

Over very low heat, slowly bring the set milk up to 100°F, stirring very gently and intermittently by hand for 10 minutes. The curds will shrink and begin to firm up (and look a bit like cottage cheese) expelling whey, known as "noros."

Turn off the heat and let rest for 5 minutes.

Gently strain the curds from the whey. In Cyprus, we just used our hands to scoop out the whey but you could also use a fine sieve and pack into cheese baskets (talarin) or pierced milk cartons lined with cloth placed on a baking sheet. Push the curds down with the back of your hand to release as much whey as possible. Reserve the whey.

Turn the cheese out and cut into ¾in-thick slices. Squeeze them gently between the palms of your hands to release excess whey, then pile on top of each other for 30 minutes. Reverse the stacking order after 15 minutes; the discs will act as self weights.

Recipe continued on the next page

When making halloumi, a by-product cheese called Anari is produced—basically a Greek ricotta. With these quantities, you'll make only a miniscule amount, but if you like ricotta cheese, you'll love this as much as the Greeks do.

To make the Anari, reheat the pan of whey until it reaches 190–195°F. Julia makes the sign of the cross before adding 1 teaspoon sea salt and 2 teaspoons white vinegar. Turn off the heat and watch the curds as they rise to the top. Remove the curds with a fine sieve or perforated spoon and eat immediately while warm, sprinkled with a little cinnamon and sugar or sugar and rose water. Alternatively, place in a small colander or sieve lined with cheesecloth. Bring the sides together, twist, and drain of excess whey for an hour. Refrigerate and use within a day.

The Greeks also mix the Anari with extra salt and pack it into a talarin or cheesecloth and hang to dry until it's hard as rock (Julia's description!). The result is a Parmesan-type cheese that's often grated over pasta.

Recipe continued

If using a cheesecloth-lined colander, fold the cloth over the curds and weigh down with a plate topped with cans. Leave the curds in the colander placed over a bowl to drain of excess whey for 30 minutes. While the halloumi's draining you can make Anari—see left. Once you have your Anari (and by the way, you can just leave that step out if you don't want it!) continue with the halloumi.

Add the reserved whey to the pan and slowly heat to 190°F. Unmold the halloumi and cut into slices and squeeze as on page 35.

At this stage, Julia makes a sign of the cross over the pan (it's a very religious affair, making halloumi), before adding the slices. They need to be kept at a constant temperature for about 20 minutes or until they rise to the surface. Give them an occasional gentle stir during this time. Remove the halloumi with a slotted spoon to a cloth-lined baking sheet for 5 minutes, then gently squeeze between your palms.

Sprinkle the sea salt and dried mint (or a little fresh mint if you prefer) over both sides of each halloumi and fold in half.

You can eat immediately or store in the refrigerator for a day, or up to a week if preserved in brine (see below). You can even freeze it, but I think once you've tasted how amazing this fresh halloumi is, it'll be gone within days!

To make a brine solution, dissolve ⅓ cup sea salt in 2 cups boiling water. Add 2 cups of the reserved whey, mix, and cool. Once cool, pour over the cooled halloumi and refrigerate, making sure the halloumi is submerged in the brine. Ziplock or freezer bags are good for this. Remember to rinse the halloumi before using or it'll be too salty.

*Note
The amount of rennet you need really depends on the brand of rennet you use, so it's advisable to check the guidelines on the package first.

thecheesemaker.com and getculture.com both stock conical cheese molds, baskets, cheesecloth, rennet, and digital thermometers.

OUZO AND LEMON CURED SALMON

This is a good dish for entertaining. Rather than buying smoked salmon, cure your own. You're keeping the freshness of the salmon, but adding a little zing and depth. The anise and lemon complement each other and will cut through the fattiness of the salmon, adding an interesting Greek twist. You'll need to let the salmon marinate for a minimum of two days, maximum of four.

There are so many delicious ways to serve this salmon— see Serving Suggestions.

Serves 4–8

18oz skin-on salmon fillet, pin-boned
1 cup sea salt
1 cup superfine sugar
finely grated zest of 1 lemon
1 teaspoon freshly ground black pepper
2 tablespoons fennel seeds, crushed
⅓ cup ouzo

Double-check the salmon for any bones that may have been missed and pull out with tweezers. At the restaurant we use special fish tweezers, but at home it's usually my eyebrow ones!

Lay a length of plastic wrap (long enough to cover the salmon) on a work surface and top with another.

Mix together the salt, sugar, lemon zest, pepper, and fennel seeds and set aside. Place the salmon, skin-side down, on top of the plastic wrap and drizzle with the ouzo. Cover the salmon flesh with the salt mixture, remembering the sides, and carefully wrap up tightly, being careful not to lose the ouzo. Place on a rimmed baking sheet and top with another, then weigh down using cans. Refrigerate for a minimum of two days or maximum of four. Remove the salmon from the plastic wrap, rinse off the marinade, and pat dry with paper towels. Depending on your knife skills, you may want to wrap the salmon in plastic wrap again and freeze for a couple of hours before slicing. (Freezing a little will firm up the flesh and you may find it easier to slice it wafer-thin.)

Using a carving knife, finely slice the salmon on the diagonal.

Serving suggestions: Serve on toast spread with Feta Curd (page 102) and top with Pickled Vegetables (page 154) or shaved raw fennel and crispy capers. Smear a little White Bean, Artichoke, and Basil Hummus (page 136) over the surface of a plate or platter, and top with some shaved fennel dressed in a little Ouzo Lemon Dressing (page 161) followed by some slices of salmon, and scatter with pea shoots and violas. Or serve in a chunky sourdough sandwich with cucumber and Ouzo Mayonnaise (page 43), or with a pile of Ouzo Celeriac and Fennel Remoulade (page 148) and some crusty bread... the list is endless!

CALAMARI, EGGPLANT, AND TOMATO BRAISE

Calamari should be cooked slow and low or fast and high to prevent it from being chewy. A cooked eggplant and tomato salad is one of my favorite dishes and I thought it would be interesting to add the calamari. This is a healthy mix of Mediterranean flavors at their best! Serve with a crisp green salad and pita or with Tomato Bulgur Pilaf (page 147) or Feta Polenta (page 141) on the side.

Variations: Try adding peas instead of eggplant, omitting the spices, and adding some chopped dill and cinnamon to flavor.

Serves 8

2 eggplants, weighing 14oz–1lb in total
2 tablespoons olive oil
3 garlic cloves, finely chopped
2 tablespoons tomato paste
a good pinch of dried red pepper flakes
1 teaspoon paprika
2 teaspoons ground cumin
1lb 2oz vine-ripened plum tomatoes, peeled and chopped
a pinch of sugar
1lb 2oz calamari, cleaned and sliced into ½in rings, the tentacles cut in half
juice of 1 lemon
1 bunch of finely chopped fresh flat-leaf parsley
8 Kalamata olives, pitted and chopped (optional)
sea salt and freshly ground black pepper

Preheat the oven to 425°F. Pierce the eggplants all over with a fork and place on a baking sheet in the oven for 30–45 minutes, until completely soft.

Meanwhile, gently heat the olive oil in a large saucepan. Add the garlic to the pan off the heat (to avoid burning), swirl the oil around a little, then add the tomato paste, pepper flakes, paprika, and cumin. Return to the heat, stirring constantly for 1 minute. Add the tomatoes and sugar and bring almost to a boil, then reduce the heat and simmer for 5 minutes before adding the calamari. Cook over low heat for 40 minutes, stirring occasionally, after which time the calamari should be almost tender. Set the pan aside while you prepare the eggplants.

Once they are cool enough to handle, cut each eggplant in half lengthwise then, holding onto the stem, scoop the flesh from the skin using a spoon. Roughly chop the flesh and place in a colander to drain away any bitter juices. Add the eggplant pieces to the tomato and calamari mixture and return to the heat. Cook over low heat for another 30 minutes, stirring occasionally. The calamari should be meltingly tender and the sauce will have thickened.

Stir in the lemon juice, parsley, and olives, if using, and season to taste with salt and pepper. Serve hot or at room temperature.

ZUCCHINI-COATED CALAMARI

One day I was talking to Elena, my Greek chef friend, about food and ingredients, like we always do. I had this idea that it would be lovely to coat calamari with keftede mix and I got really excited about it, so here it is! I called it calamari because I liked the repetition of the "c"— it sounds so much better than "Zucchini-coated Squid"! Serve with some Tzatziki (page 128) or Lemon and Dill Braised Fava beans (page 135).

Serves 4

For the coating:
10oz zucchini, trimmed and grated
3 tablespoons grated onion
⅓ cup feta, crumbled
½ cup grated Parmesan or Kefalotyri
2½ tablespoons chopped fresh flat-leaf parsley
2½ tablespoons chopped fresh dill
2½ tablespoons chopped fresh mint
¼ cup fresh bread crumbs
3 free-range eggs, beaten

14oz cleaned calamari
vegetable oil, for frying
all-purpose flour, for dusting
sea salt and freshly ground black pepper
lemon wedges, to serve

To make the coating, blanch the zucchini in boiling water for 2 minutes, then drain. Place in a clean cloth and squeeze dry by twisting the opposite ends. Place in a bowl and combine with the grated onion, cheeses, herbs, and bread crumbs. Whisk in the beaten eggs to form a batter.

Cut open the calamari lengthwise and then cut into pieces about 2½ x 1½in in size.

Preheat some vegetable oil in a heavy-bottomed saucepan or in a deep-fat fryer to 350°F.

Put the flour in a shallow bowl and season with salt and pepper. Dredge the calamari with the flour, shake off any excess, then coat in the zucchini mixture.

Carefully lower the calamari, in batches, into the hot oil and cook until golden and crisp. Drain on paper towels, sprinkle with a little salt, and serve immediately with lemon wedges.

OUZO MAYONNAISE
SHRIMP COCKTAIL

This is a retro classic with a Greek twist that always makes me smile!

You could use crawfish tails, large prawns, lobster meat, or cooked octopus (see page 49) as an alternative to the shrimp.

Serves 4

14oz cooked jumbo shrimp, shell on
¾ cup Ouzo Mayonnaise (see opposite)
2 tablespoons chopped fresh tarragon or dill
1 tablespoon lemon juice
sea salt and freshly ground black pepper
1 bunch Romaine lettuce, or ½ head iceberg lettuce
   (I prefer the Romaine leaf for garnish)
½ bulb of fennel, finely sliced widthwise
1 avocado, diced
paprika, for sprinkling

<u>To serve:</u>
1 lemon, cut into wedges
crusty bread and butter (optional)

Peel all but 4 of the shrimp, cut them in half, and combine with the mayonnaise, herbs, and lemon juice and mix thoroughly. Season with a little salt and pepper.

Select 4 good-looking Romaine leaves and set aside for the garnish. Shred the crisp inner leaves and mix with the fennel.

Place a Romaine lettuce leaf down the side of each of 4 glasses and place the lettuce mixture in the bottom, followed by some avocado. Spoon the prawn mayo over the top and sprinkle with a little paprika to add that retro touch! Garnish with the remaining shrimp and lemon wedges and serve immediately, preferably with buttered crusty bread!

OUZO MAYONNAISE

Don't be tempted to make this with extra-virgin olive oil. It's too harsh and overpowering for mayonnaise and also a waste of money. One option would be to use 1 cup of something like a grapeseed or sunflower oil plus 2 tablespoons of extra-virgin olive oil. For a quick version, you could of course add a dash of ouzo to a store-bought mayonnaise.

Makes about 1 cup

2 free-range egg yolks, at
   room temperature
2 teaspoons Dijon mustard
sea salt
1 cup + 2 tablepoons light olive oil
3 tablespoons ouzo
2 teaspoons lemon juice

Whisk the yolks, mustard, and a pinch of salt together in a bowl with a hand-held blender (or by hand) until thick—if you sit your bowl on a damp kitchen towel it'll stop it from spinning around. (Alternatively, you can make the mayonnaise in a blender.) While whisking slowly, add the oil a little at a time until it forms a thick consistency. Stir in the ouzo and the lemon juice. Season with a little sea salt and refrigerate until required. Use within 3 days.

Variations: To make a lighter mayonnaise, stir through a tablespoonful or two of Greek yogurt. You could also add chopped fresh dill or tarragon, anchovies, or olives and some crushed garlic and use on new potatoes for a salad.

TARAMASALATA AND SALT COD CROQUETTES

My chef friend José Pizarro and I talked about cooking a supper club together and combining our love of Greek and Spanish food and I automatically thought how great his salt cod croquettas (which I think are the best in London) would be with taramasalata. You'll need to start this recipe 24 hours ahead in order to soak the salt cod. You can either use homemade Taramasalata (page 129), or a good-quality bought one. Serve hot with garlic and dill yogurt, Ouzo Mayonnaise (page 43), or extra taramasalata.

Makes 32 croquettes

12oz salt cod (*bacalao*)
1lb 10oz red skinned potatoes
¾ cup Taramasalata (page 129)
2 garlic cloves, finely chopped
2 tablespoons chopped fresh flat-leaf parsley
2 tablespoons chopped fresh dill
zest and juice of ½ lemon
½ teaspoon cayenne pepper
sea salt
1 cup all-purpose flour, for dusting
2 free-range eggs, beaten
2 cups fresh bread crumbs
vegetable or sunflower oil, for frying

Soak the salt cod in cold water for 24 hours, changing the water regularly. Peel and cut the potatoes into even-sized pieces and boil in salted water until tender, about 20 minutes. Drain well and mash or pass through a ricer.

Meanwhile, cook the salt cod. Place the fish in a pan, cover with cold water, and heat until the water simmers. Cook the fish until it's tender to touch, about 10–15 minutes, depending on the thickness of the fish. (Be careful not to let the water boil or the fish will become tough.) Drain, cool, and flake the fish, discarding the skin and bones. Add the flaked cod, taramasalata, garlic, herbs, lemon zest, and juice to the potatoes, and mix until well combined. Season with the cayenne and taste for salt.

Sprinkle a cutting board or work surface with a little flour and roll the mixture into a long cylinder about 1¼in in diameter. Cut into 32 equal pieces, about 1½in long. Transfer to a baking sheet lined with parchment paper and let chill in the fridge for an hour.

Dip each croquette into flour, then beaten egg, and then roll in the bread crumbs to coat. (I always use my right hand for the dry mixtures and my left for the egg.) Refrigerate until required. You can prepare the croquettes up to two days in advance (in which case, refrigerate uncovered).

Preheat the oven to 325°F. Heat some oil to 350°F in a heavy-bottomed pan or deep-fryer. Carefully lower the croquettes, in batches, into the oil and fry until golden brown. Cook no more than six at a time, then drain on paper towels and keep warm in the oven while you cook the remainder. Serve hot with the dip of your choice.

SCALLOPS, GREEK SAUSAGE, (SOUTZOUKI) AND WATERMELON

Soutzouki is one of the best Greek sausages you will ever taste! It's a deliciously spicy and piquant beef and lamb sausage flavored with cumin, pepper, garlic, and sumac and shaped like a horseshoe. Paired with chilled, refreshing watermelon, sweet and sour oregano dressing, and seared plump scallops, it's a match made in heaven. Try replacing soutzouki with a picante cooking chorizo or a spiced Loukaniko sausage. Soutzouki is available in Greek and Turkish delicatessens.

Serves 4

1 small watermelon
7oz soutzouki, peeled and cut into ⅛in slices
a handful of mixed leaves, such as mizuna, arugula, and dandelion
Raisin Oregano Dressing (page 30)
a splash of olive oil
8 even-sized scallops
sea salt and freshly ground black pepper
shiso sprouts and micro cilantro, to garnish (optional)

Slice the top and bottom off the watermelon and stand upright on a work surface. Remove the skin as you would that of an orange, cutting from top to bottom to reveal the melon flesh. Discard the skin and cut the flesh into ¾in thick slices. Cut each slice into rectangular blocks 3½ x 2 x ¾in then put in the fridge to chill.

Preheat the broiler to medium-hot. Place the soutzouki slices on a baking sheet, then place under the broiler for 3 minutes on each side.

Place a piece of chilled watermelon in the center of each plate and top each with a few leaves, followed by a tablespoon of Raisin Oregano dressing.

Place a medium, nonstick frying pan over medium heat and add a splash of oil. Season the scallops with salt and pepper and carefully place in the pan. Increase the heat to high and sear the scallops for 1 minute on either side, until caramelized. (I find that the easiest way to do this is to place the scallops clockwise in a circle, enabling you to turn them over in the correct order.) While the scallops are cooking, remove the soutzouki from the broiler.

Place two slices of soutzouki on top of the melon, followed by the scallops. Garnish with shiso sprouts and micro cilantro, if using, and serve immediately.

Use the leftover watermelon to make a feta, watermelon, and mint salad or the Watermelon Mahalepi on page 190.

OLIVE, CAPER, AND HERB STUFFED SARDINES WITH ARTICHOKE SALAD

Fresh sardines are a favorite of mine; I honestly get excited about them being in season (I know, odd!). Not only are they full of flavor, they're rich in omega-3 and economical too. It was really hard to decide on just one recipe to include using whole sardines. In the end I opted for this one, a kind of reversed sardines on toast. Salty olives, acidic, sour capers, and herbs add freshness and depth to these oily beauties.

Ask the fishmonger to gut, scale, and butterfly the sardines for you, or follow my instructions.

Serves 4

8 small/4 large fresh sardines
olive oil, for drizzling

For the stuffing:
½ teaspoon dried red pepper flakes
½ cup fresh bread crumbs
¼ cup pitted and chopped green olives
¼ cup capers, roughly chopped
2 tablespoons chopped fresh flat-leaf parsley
2 tablespoons chopped fresh oregano
1 garlic clove, peeled and crushed
zest of ½ lemon
sea salt and freshly ground black pepper
a glug of olive oil

For the salad:
6 cooked artichoke hearts in olive oil, cut into wedges
a handful of fresh flat-leaf parsley or arugula leaves
5 tablespoons extra-virgin olive oil
2 tablespoons red or white wine vinegar
2 tablespoons lemon juice

Preheat the oven to 375°F.

I prefer to leave the sardine heads on, but if you wish to cut them off, do so before you butterfly as follows: Hold the fish in one hand and, using kitchen scissors or a small knife, cut the belly open from head to tail. Pull out the guts, discard, and place the fish flesh-side flat down on a cutting board. Using your thumb, press down firmly on the backbone from head to tail. Turn

the fish over and carefully pull the backbone away from the flesh, working from the head toward the tail. Using scissors, cut the backbone away and remove any small bones left behind.

For the stuffing, place the pepper flakes, bread crumbs, olives, capers, herbs, garlic, and lemon zest in a bowl. Add a pinch of salt and pepper and mix in a glug of olive oil to combine. Lay the sardines on a cutting board, flesh side up.

Preheat a grill pan while you spoon the stuffing evenly into the cavities of each sardine. Fold the sardines closed, drizzle with a little olive oil, and season lightly. Place on a medium-hot grill pan and cook the sardines for about 2 minutes on each side until cooked through.

To make the salad, toss together the artichokes, parsley or arugula, olive oil, vinegar, and lemon juice, and serve with the hot sardines as part of a selection of small plates.

Variations: To vary the stuffing, you could replace the lemon zest and juice with orange, or replace 3 tablespoons of the bread crumbs with some toasted pine nuts and Parmesan or grated feta. Alternatively, serve with the White Bean Salad on page 136. If you don't want to stuff the sardines, leave them whole, sear, and then roast in a preheated oven for 5 minutes at 350°F, drizzled with olive oil, chile, capers, olives, herbs, garlic, and lemon zest. Serve with a little salad or on toasted bread, drizzling with the pan juices for a decadent version of sardines on toast.

OCTOPUS WITH FENNEL AND BARLEY SALAD

Octopus is something you tend to eat when you're abroad and forget about at home, but we should eat more of it because it's so delicious and, cooked correctly, it's meltingly tender. The barley adds a nutty texture to mix it all up.

Serves 4–6

For the octopus:
1 medium octopus, about 2¼lb, cleaned (page 78)
2 teaspoons fennel seeds
a pinch of dried red pepper flakes
a glug of olive oil

For the fennel purée:
1 large bulb of fennel
a good glug of olive oil
juice of ½ lemon
sea salt

For the salad:
¾ cup barley
a good glug of olive oil
2 small red onions, finely chopped
1 small bulb of fennel, finely chopped
micro fennel sprouts if available, or use fennel fronds
sea salt
1 lemon, cut into wedges, to serve

For the fennel seed dressing:
2 tablespoons fennel seeds
2 small garlic cloves
2 teaspoons sea salt
¼ cup olive oil
¼ cup extra-virgin olive oil
¼ cup red wine vinegar
¼ cup reserved octopus cooking liquid

Preheat the oven to 300°F. Select a roasting pan or Dutch oven in which the octopus will fit snugly. Place the octopus on the bottom, scatter with the fennel seeds and pepper flakes, and drizzle with a glug of olive oil. Cover with foil and cook for about 2 hours, until tender when pierced with the tip of a knife. Avoid overcooking the octopus as this can make it tough. Continue with the fennel purée and salad in the meantime.

To make the fennel purée, cut the fennel into thin wedges; toss with olive oil and salt and place on one side of a large, double-layered piece of foil. Fold the foil over to form a loose package and seal the edges. Place on a baking sheet and cook in the oven with the octopus for about 50 minutes, or until tender. Transfer to a blender and process with the lemon juice and a dash of olive oil until smooth. Season with a little sea salt if needed, then set aside at room temperature.

To make the salad, begin by dry-roasting the barley in a frying pan for about 2 minutes over medium heat until nutty and fragrant. Transfer to a saucepan, cover with water, and bring to a boil. Reduce the heat and simmer until tender, about 30 minutes. Transfer to a colander and refresh under cold running water. Drain and transfer to a bowl.

Heat the olive oil in a frying pan, add the onions, and cook over medium heat until softened and caramelized (about 10 minutes), then add to the barley. Return the pan to the heat, adding a glug more of oil; when the oil's hot, add the fennel and cook over high heat until the fennel is colored and softened. Add to the barley and onions and mix well.

Once tender, remove the octopus from the oven. Pass the cooking liquid through a fine sieve and reserve. Cut the octopus into individual tentacles. (If making ahead of time, store them under the cooking liquid.)

To make the dressing, lightly toast the fennel seeds in a pan over medium heat until aromatic. Once cool, transfer to a mortar and pestle and crush with the garlic and sea salt. Transfer to a small bowl and whisk in the oils, vinegar, and octopus cooking liquid.

When you're ready to serve, preheat a grill pan or outdoor grill, drizzle the octopus tentacles with a little oil, and cook for about 5 minutes until charred and the thinnest ends of the tentacles are crisp. To assemble, dress the barley salad with a generous amount of the dressing and season to taste. Smear a little fennel purée over the center of each plate and top with the barley salad. Add the octopus and serve immediately, drizzled with dressing and garnished with micro fennel sprouts, if available, and a wedge of lemon.

SARDINE KEFTEDES

These are great served cold in a sandwich with skordalia, vine-ripened tomatoes, and fresh basil—it adds a whole new meaning to a fish finger sandwich! I like to serve mine with Lemon Parsley Salad (page 147) and a little Skordalia (page 130), Taramasalata (page 129), or dill yogurt.

Variations: Omit the Kefalotyri and add ⅓ cup of crumbled feta and 2 tablespoons of grated onion.

Makes 12

1 x 14oz can of chickpeas, drained
¼ cup fresh flat-leaf parsley, chopped
3 tablespoons fresh mint, finely chopped
2 tablespoons tahini
2 x 3½oz cans of sardines, drained, backbones removed
a pinch of ground cinnamon
1 teaspoon ground cumin
½ teaspoon paprika
⅓ cup Kefalotyri, Parmesan, or Pecorino
1 free-range egg
sea salt and freshly ground black pepper
¾ cup fresh bread crumbs
all-purpose flour, for dusting
olive oil, for frying
sumac, to sprinkle
lemon wedges, to serve (optional)

Put the chickpeas, herbs, and tahini in a food processor and pulse until the chickpeas have broken up a little. Transfer to a bowl. Add the sardines, flaking them into pieces by hand, then the spices, cheese, egg, and some salt and pepper. Mix well, adding the bread crumbs to combine.

Divide the mixture into 12 and roll into balls, dusting in the flour. Place on a baking sheet lined with parchment paper and refrigerate, uncovered, for a couple of hours to firm up.

Heat a little olive oil in a frying pan over medium heat, slightly flatten the keftedes so they'll cook evenly, and pan-fry until golden on each side (about 3 minutes per side). You could deep-fry if you prefer, at 325°F for 2–3 minutes, turning once. Drain on paper towels, sprinkle with salt and sumac, and serve immediately or at room temperature, with lemon wedges on the side, if you wish.

PICKLED SQUAB

One of my earliest childhood memories was eating pickled squab. My dad (pictured) used to take me shooting, and we'd often return with squab, pheasants, and rabbits, much to my mother and sister's horror. My dad would pickle the squab. It's not the most attractive of meats, gray in color, but delicious in taste. Here's my version, using Chardonnay vinegar. I serve this at room temperature with the Cherry Relish below, Almond Crumbs (page 154), Celeriac Purée (page 146), and a few watercress leaves. The squab will keep for up to a week in the pickling liquid. This recipe could also be made using wood pigeon or partridge; check with your local butcher.

As a guest in any Greek house, you'll be offered a "spoon sweet" made from fruits or vegetables and traditionally served with a glass of cold water. A tray arrives laden with an array of sweet preserves to which guests help themselves with a spoon. After eating the sweet, you place the spoon in a glass of water so any remaining syrup can sweeten the water which you then drink. It really is quite a ritual and the Greeks get quite offended if you don't eat at least one spoon sweet!

Cherries, nestled in an incredibly sweet syrup, make marvelous spoon sweets. Here's my not-so-sweet cherry relish that's a perfect accompaniment to any braised or roasted red meat, or the Pickled Squab above. It's also delicious served alongside Honeyed Fried Feta (page 29).

Serves 4

4 squab breasts
sea salt
glug of olive oil
⅔ cup water
1 shallot, halved
1 celery rib, halved
2 garlic cloves, finely sliced
1 bay leaf
10 black peppercorns
3 sprigs of thyme
1 cup Chardonnay vinegar or white wine vinegar

Season the squab breasts with sea salt. Heat the oil in a frying pan and sear them on either side until colored. Set aside.

Bring a large pan of salted water to a boil. Add the squab and simmer for 3 minutes. Turn off the heat, cover, and let cool.

Meanwhile, heat the water and the remaining ingredients in a non-reactive pan and bring to a boil. Turn off the heat and set aside. Remove the cooled squab from its water, pat dry, and sprinkle with sea salt. Place in a sterilized jar and pour in the strained, cooled pickling liquid to cover. Seal the surface with a glug of olive oil and refrigerate overnight before serving.

CHERRY RELISH

2 tablespoons olive oil
2 shallots, finely chopped
1 tablespoon superfine sugar
2 tablespoons cider or red wine vinegar
2 tablespoons Mavrodaphne, Commandaria, or port
1 star anise
1 small cinnamon stick
1 strip of orange rind
¾lb cherries, pitted

Heat the olive oil in a saucepan. Add the shallots and cook until softened. Add the sugar, vinegar, Mavrodaphne, Commandaria, or port, star anise, cinnamon stick, and orange rind. Stir over low heat until the sugar dissolves.

Add the cherries and increase the heat until boiling, then reduce to a simmer for about 20 minutes, stirring occasionally, until the cherry relish becomes "jammy." Remove from the heat and let cool. This will keep for up to 1 week in the fridge.

PICKLED CHICKEN

I was telling my dear friend (and recipe tester!) Elena how much I loved pickled squab and how it reminded me of my childhood. She said that she felt the same way about pickled chicken! That set my mind racing; we never ate pickled chicken in our house, only squab. It was her Aunty Frosoulla who made it. Unfortunately, Frosoulla is no longer with us, so this is my version, just for her and Elena. I hope I've done her proud.

Try serving it with Lemon and Dill Braised Fava beans (page 135) and Tzatziki (page 128), or pile into a pita bread with salad and Ouzo Mayonnaise (page 43).

To sterilize your jar, run it through the dishwasher, then remove and let cool before immediately filling. Never fill a hot jar with cold food or a cold jar with hot food, otherwise the glass may shatter.

Makes 1 large jar

1 x 4½lb free-range chicken, at room temperature
2 celery ribs, roughly chopped
1 onion, roughly chopped
1 carrot, roughly chopped
4 garlic cloves
4 dried bay leaves (or 3 fresh)
20 black peppercorns
1 dried chile (optional)
2 strips of lemon zest, pith removed
2½ cups white wine vinegar
3 sprigs of thyme
1 tablespoon coriander seeds
10 celery leaves, shredded
¾ cup water
sea salt

You will need a large sterilized jar.

Remove any giblets from the chicken and place it in a large stockpot with the celery, onion, carrot, two of the garlic cloves, two of the bay leaves, and half the peppercorns. Add enough cold water to cover the chicken by an inch or two.

Place over medium-high heat and bring almost to a boil, then reduce the heat so the water is simmering gently. Cook for 1½ hours, skimming regularly and topping off with water if necessary to keep the chicken covered. Remove from the heat, cover, and let stand for an hour.

Remove the chicken from the liquid, pull the meat from the bones, and place in the sterilized jar. Strain the liquid through a fine sieve, discarding the veggies, etc., skim off the fat, and reserve for making soup.

Slice the remaining garlic and place in a non-reactive saucepan with the remaining bay leaves and peppercorns, the chile if using, lemon zest, vinegar, thyme, coriander seeds, celery leaves, and water. Bring to a boil and cook for 5 minutes. Remove from the heat and let cool before pouring over the chicken meat to cover. Seal the surface with a little olive oil and refrigerate for 24 hours before serving. The chicken will keep under the pickling liquid for a week.

Serve the chicken at room temperature sprinkled with sea salt.

CURED DUCK "HAM"

You'll need to be patient, but hopefully you'll agree the wait will be worth it. There's nothing more rewarding than curing your own meat, and duck is a great place to start. In Cyprus there's a speciality called Tsamarella, which is salt and oregano cured goat meat. It's made from the thigh meat, cut into strips, immersed in salt and oregano, and left to dry in the sun for 7–10 days. The taste is delicious, pleasantly gamey and a little spicy, far better than its particularly uninviting appearance. But for now, here's a simple cured duck breast that needs no sun! If you're butchering whole ducks, use the legs for Duck Shepherd's Pie (page 98).

Serves 8

½ cup sea salt*
1 tablespoon granulated sugar
1 tablespoon black peppercorns, crushed
1 tablespoon finely chopped fresh thyme leaves**
2 tablespoons finely chopped fresh oregano leaves
2 large duck breasts, about 10½oz each,
   or 4 small duck breasts

Combine all the ingredients except the duck in a bowl and mix together. Lightly score the duck in a cross-hatch fashion and rub the salt mix into the meat. Wrap the duck loosely in parchment paper, place on a baking sheet, and refrigerate for four days, turning after two.

Unwrap, wipe off the salt mix, and pat dry with paper towels; truss each breast with string—as you would a parcel—leaving around a ¾in gap between each truss, with enough string left at the end of each to tie into a loop. (You could eat the duck at this stage, but the flavor intensifies when left for longer.) Suspend the duck from a shelf in the fridge (it's important that the air can circulate around the breasts) or hang in a cool cellar if you have one, ensuring the temperature doesn't exceed 39°F. Let cure for 3 weeks.

After 3 weeks, unwrap and cut a thin slice to try it; the meat should be dark, firm, and dry and the layer of fat firm and almost waxy.

Slice the duck as finely as possible and serve with some ripe figs, shaved Kefalotyri or Parmesan, a few arugula leaves, and a drizzle of honey, or alternatively with some Dried Fig Leaf Pasta Rags (see page 116).

Variations: add chopped rosemary, fennel seeds, coriander seeds, juniper, or allspice berries for additional flavor.

*It is important to use sea salt as it has natural curing agents, in addition to sodium chloride, that rock salt doesn't have. Curing small cuts of meat such as duck breasts needs about 20 percent salt in proportion to the weight of the meat.

**As well as adding flavor, thyme contains antibacterial agents that protect the duck from contamination as it cures.

QUAIL, THEIR EGGS, AND OKRA

I have to admit that the first time I ate okra, I hated it; its slimy texture really put me off, as it does many people. Fortunately, I've learned that there's a way to make it much more enjoyable by pre-soaking it in vinegar to eliminate the "slime." In Greece, okra is sometimes salted and dried in the sun. It's not uncommon to serve eggs with okra and so I thought it would be interesting to use quail's eggs, and then I thought, why not include the whole bird! You could just serve the okra at room temperature or chilled as part a selection of small plates.

Serves 4

9oz small okra, stem ends trimmed
¼ cup white wine vinegar
sea salt and freshly ground black pepper
3 tablespoons olive oil
1 small onion, halved and thinly sliced
2 garlic cloves, finely chopped
a pinch of ground allspice
a pinch of dried red pepper flakes
a pinch of superfine sugar
3 tomatoes, peeled and roughly chopped
1 tablespoon lemon juice
2 tablespoons chopped fresh flat-leaf parsley
1 tablespoon chopped fresh cilantro
4–8 quail eggs, depending on how hungry you are!

extra-virgin olive oil, to serve

For the quail:
4 quails, spatchcocked (see page 87 for how
   to spatchcock, or ask your butcher to do it)
1 garlic clove
a pinch of sea salt
¼ cup olive oil
2 thyme sprigs, picked
2 teaspoons finely grated lemon zest

Place the okra in a bowl, toss with the vinegar and a pinch of salt, and leave for about 45 minutes, but no more than an hour. Rinse and drain then set aside.

Meanwhile, marinate the quail. Crush the garlic with a pinch of sea salt and mix with the olive oil, thyme, and lemon zest. Rub all over the quails and let marinate for about 1½ hours while you watch TV, check your emails, or prepare the other ingredients!

Preheat the oven to 350°F. Heat a glug of olive oil in an ovenproof frying pan, add the onion, and cook until softened, about 8 minutes. Add the garlic, spices, and okra and continue to cook for about 3 minutes, stirring occasionally. Add the sugar, the tomatoes, and a pinch of sea salt and simmer for 30–35 minutes, covered but stirring occasionally, until the okra is tender when pierced. (Add a splash of water if it looks a little too dry.)

Start to cook the quails 5 minutes before the okra is ready. Preheat a broiler or grill pan, season the quails with a little sea salt, and cook, skin-side up (or down, if grilling), until browned, about 3–5 minutes on each side. Let rest.

Stir the lemon juice and herbs into the okra and season to taste. Break the quail's eggs on top of the okra and place under the broiler, if it's on, or cover the pan with a lid or plate and cook in the oven until the whites are set (about 3 minutes).

Halve the quails and serve in the pan with the okra and eggs, drizzled with extra-virgin olive oil.

Variations: Add a few cooked and sliced new potatoes to the okra for a more substantial dish. Or omit the quails and eggs and serve with pan-fried sea bass or red snapper fillets. You can also use hen's eggs if you prefer—just cook them for a little longer.

RABBIT RILLETTES

I think rabbit makes a great alternative to chicken, if not better. The Greeks eat a lot of rabbit and this is a twist on the French pork rillette, with a little added Greek spice. Another great way to serve rillettes is to spread on hot toasted bread and top with sautéed porcinis or pine mushrooms.

Variation: Sometimes I like to add a splash of red wine vinegar to the rillettes mixture.

Serves 4–6

For the confit:
2 rabbit legs
1 tablespoon sea or rock salt
3 sprigs of thyme
2 garlic cloves, crushed
1lb 2oz duck fat
1 cinnamon stick
3 teaspoons finely chopped fresh oregano
a pinch of ground cinnamon
finely grated zest of 1 lemon, and juice, to taste
sea salt and freshly ground black pepper
a pinch of freshly grated nutmeg

To serve:
8 Anise and Sesame Crackers (page 166), or toasted
    ciabatta/Greek bread
4 figs, quartered
honey, to drizzle
lamb's lettuce or mache, to garnish (optional)

To make the confit, place the rabbit on a plastic or non-reactive tray, or line a baking sheet with plastic wrap. Scatter with the salt, thyme, and garlic, loosely cover with plastic wrap, and refrigerate for a minimum of 8 hours or overnight. When you're ready to cook, preheat the oven to 300°F.

Rinse the salt from the rabbit with cold water and pat dry. Place in a roasting pan or Dutch oven that will hold the rabbit snugly and is deep enough for the legs to be covered with the fat. Cover the legs with the duck fat and the cinnamon stick and then place a sheet of parchment paper on top. Cover with foil to seal, then place in the oven. Cook for about 3 hours or until the meat is falling from the bone. Set aside until the legs are cool enough to handle, then tear the meat from the bones, discarding the bones and cinnamon sticks, but reserving the liquid.

Shred the meat finely using two forks and put in a large bowl. Add enough of the fat and a little of the cooking liquid (this settles at the bottom and it's bursting with rich, salty, fatty flavors) to moisten the meat; add the oregano, cinnamon, and lemon zest and season with salt and pepper and a little nutmeg. Add a squeeze of lemon juice to taste; cover and refrigerate for an hour.

Remove from the fridge 15 minutes before serving. Spread the rillettes on the crackers or toasted bread, arrange the figs on top, drizzle over a little honey, and garnish with lamb's lettuce, if using.

If you're making the rillettes ahead of time, pack firmly into ramekins, Mason jars, or a terrine dish and seal the surface with the melted duck fat. The rillettes will keep in the fridge for up to 2 weeks. Remaining fat can be refrigerated for up to a month and used for roasting potatoes.

GREEK SPICED CHICKEN LIVERS

I admit I'm not a great fan of chicken livers, unless they are in a paté or spiced, as in this recipe. They are big and bold enough to match strong flavors and spices. Serve with Tahini Sauce (page 160), or as an accompaniment to tabbouleh and Sumac Flatbread (page 159). Alternatively, serve with a few toasted pine nuts sprinkled on top and some plump soaked raisins—just as delicious.

Serves 4

1lb 2oz chicken livers, cleaned of sinews and
    ideally soaked in milk for 4–10 hours
all-purpose flour, for dusting
sea salt and freshly ground black pepper
1½ cups bread crumbs
½ cup freshly grated Kefalotyri, Parmesan, or Pecorino
3 tablespoons sesame seeds
1 tablespoon finely chopped fresh thyme leaves or
    3 teaspoons dried
1 tablespoon finely chopped fresh oregano leaves or
    3 teaspoons dried
finely grated zest of 1 lemon
2 teaspoons ground cinnamon
3 teaspoons ground cumin
2 free-range eggs, beaten
olive oil, for frying

To serve:
sumac, to sprinkle (optional)
1 lemon, quartered
Tahini Sauce (page 160)

Soaking the chicken livers in milk is optional but it helps to remove any bitterness. Drain the livers and pat dry.

Season the flour generously with salt and pepper. Mix the bread crumbs with the cheese, sesame seeds, herbs, lemon zest, and spices. Dust the chicken livers in the flour, shake off any excess, then dip in the beaten egg and coat in the bread crumbs. I always use my right hand for the dry mixes—i.e. flour and bread crumbs—and my left for the egg; that way, I only coat the chicken livers and not my hands! If preparing in advance, refrigerate for 24 hours, uncovered, on a baking sheet.

Heat the oil in a large frying pan and shallow-fry the livers over medium heat until golden on each side, about 2–3 minutes. Depending on the size of your pan, you may need to cook these in batches. Drain on paper towels and season with salt, sprinkle with sumac, and serve immediately with lemon wedges and the Tahini Sauce.

GREEK EGG

This is my take on the comforting classic Scotch egg with a Greek twist! It's a real treat to have one with an oozing soft yolk. Mint, parsley, and cinnamon add a Greek flavor to the egg. Serve hot, cold, or at room temperature with tomato chutney or Ouzo Mayonnaise (page 43).

Variations: Try using half lamb, half pork sausage to vary. To add a little heat, try whisking 1 tablespoon of English mustard into the beaten eggs. You could also mix the sausage meat with a little grated Kefalotyri.

Makes 6

6 free-range eggs
a dash of vinegar
14oz good-quality Cumberland or other pork sausage, skins discarded
2 scallions, finely chopped
2 tablespoons finely chopped fresh flat-leaf parsley
1 tablespoon finely chopped fresh mint
1 teaspoon ground cinnamon or mace
a few drops of Worcestershire sauce
⅔ cup all-purpose flour, plus extra for dusting
a splash of milk
sea salt and freshly ground black pepper
1½ cups fresh white bread crumbs or Panko crumbs (for a crunchier crumb)
2 tablespoons sesame seeds (optional)
vegetable or sunflower oil, for deep-frying

Put 4 of the eggs in a saucepan, add a dash of vinegar (this will help to set the whites if they crack during cooking), and cover with cold water. Bring to a boil, turn down the heat, and simmer for 5 minutes only; carefully remove the eggs and plunge into ice-cold water; let chill for at least 10 minutes, then carefully peel.

Mix the sausage meat with the scallions, herbs, cinnamon, and Worcestershire sauce. Divide into four balls and flatten into patties large enough to encase the egg; you can do this by hand (a little flour on your hands helps) or by placing the meat patties between two floured sheets of plastic wrap and rolling with a rolling pin.

Beat the two remaining eggs together with a splash of milk and place in a shallow bowl. Put the flour in a second bowl and season with salt and pepper. Place the bread crumbs and sesame seeds, if using, together into a third bowl. Arrange in an assembly line. To assemble, dust each boiled egg in a little flour then wrap evenly in the prepared sausage mixture, molding with your hands to form an egg shape. Dip the sausage-coated eggs in flour, beaten egg, then bread crumb-sesame mixture, re-molding them if necessary.

Preheat about 4in of oil to 300°F in a large, heavy-bottomed saucepan or deep-fat fryer. Cook the eggs for approximately 5–8 minutes, turning them every so often until they are crisp and golden. Remove with a slotted spoon and drain on paper towels.

SHARING &
FULLER PLATES

TOMATO AND STRING BEAN BAKLAVA

This savory baklava is delicious eaten hot with roast lamb or broiled sardines, or makes an excellent vegetarian main dish, served with a purslane or watercress, olive, and caperberry salad with Ouzo Lemon Dressing (page 161). Served at room temperature, it even makes a great picnic food. For the best results, make the filling the day before to allow the flavors to infuse.

Serves 6–8 as a main dish, 8–12 as an appetizer

½ cup olive oil
2 Spanish onions, halved and finely sliced
2 garlic cloves, finely chopped
2 teaspoons ground cinnamon
5 tablespoons tomato paste
10 vine-ripened plum tomatoes, skinned and roughly chopped
1lb 2oz string beans, cut into 1½in lengths
a pinch of sugar
1 bunch finely chopped fresh dill (about 1oz), or
　2 tablespoons dried
sea salt and freshly ground black pepper
⅔ cup water
9 sheets of filo dough
7 tablespoons melted butter
½ cup Greek or Medjool dates, pitted and finely sliced
1⅔ cups feta, crumbled
6 tablespoons honey

Heat the olive oil in a large, heavy-bottomed saucepan over low heat and sauté the onions until softened and sticky; this can take up to 20 minutes. Add the garlic, cinnamon, and tomato paste and cook for another 2 minutes. Add the tomatoes and their juices and cook over medium heat for about 8 minutes, before adding the string beans, sugar, dill, a pinch of sea salt, and the water. Reduce the heat to a simmer and cook the beans for about 40 minutes, stirring occasionally, until the beans are soft and the sauce is nice and thick. Check the seasoning and cool before assembling.

Preheat the oven to 350°F. Unfold the dough and cover with a damp cloth to prevent it from drying out. Brush a baking sheet (about 12 x 8in) with melted butter. Line the pan with a sheet of filo (cut to fit if too big), brush with butter, and repeat until you have a three-layer thickness.

Spread half the tomato and bean mixture over the dough and top with half each of the dates and feta. Sandwich another three layers of filo together with melted butter and place on top. Top with the remaining tomato mixture, dates, and feta. Sandwich the remaining three filo sheets together as before and place on top.

Lightly score the top, cutting into diamonds. Brush with the remaining butter and splash with a little water. Cook for 35–45 minutes or until golden. Let cool slightly before serving, drizzling each portion with a little honey.

ZUCCHINI, CAPER, AND HERB LINGUINE

We didn't tend to eat a lot of pasta at home when I was a child as my mother is a diabetic, but I remember my dad serving spaghetti with steak in his restaurant, and it was always a real treat. I spent nine months working in Tuscany several years ago, and that totally sorted my pasta cravings out! This recipe is full of fresh flavors and takes no time to make. For an even quicker option, you can cook the zucchini with the pasta (just add 4 minutes before the end).

Variation: A lovely variation to this recipe is to cook some peeled shrimp with the capers and then add a little freshly grated lemon zest at the end. If you have the luxury of having Pickled Caper Leaves (page 153), you may want to toss a few through the pasta as well.

Serves 4–6

2 medium zucchini, trimmed
10½oz fresh linguine (dried is fine if it's all you have)
a good glug of olive oil
¼ cup + 2 tablespoons salted capers, rinsed and dried
2 garlic cloves, finely chopped
a pinch of dried red pepper flakes (optional)
½ cup chopped mint
¾ cup chopped fresh dill
¼ cup chopped fresh flat-leaf parsley
sea salt and freshly ground black pepper
7 tablespoons butter, diced
1¼ cups freshly grated Kefalotyri, Parmesan, or Pecorino

Slice the zucchini lengthwise as thinly as possible and cut into long shreds.

Cook the pasta in boiling, salted water according to the package instructions, then drain in a colander, reserving a little of the cooking water.

While the pasta is cooking, heat the olive oil in a large frying pan over medium heat, add the capers, and cook until crisp. Set aside, heat a little more oil in the pan, and cook the zucchini, garlic, and pepper flakes, if using, until they are just tender. (You may need to cook the zucchini in two batches depending on the size of your pan.)

Toss the zucchini with the drained pasta, along with the capers and herbs. Season with salt and pepper. Add the butter, ¼ cup of the reserved cooking water, and half the cheese and mix well. Serve immediately, sprinkled with the remaining cheese.

EGGPLANT SOUVLAKI WITH TAHINI SAUCE AND DUKKAH

The Greek diet has been influenced by traditions from both the East and West. In ancient times, the Persians introduced Middle Eastern foods to the Greeks, as did the Arabs, Turks, and Romans. This souvlaki is inspired by my love of Middle Eastern cuisine. Souvlaki is Greek for sword, referring to the skewers.

Variation: Substitute wedges of roasted pumpkin or squash for the eggplant.

Serves 4

2 large eggplants
olive oil, for drizzling
sea salt and freshly ground black pepper
Tahini Sauce (page 160)

For the marinade:
2 garlic cloves, crushed
4 teaspoons ground cumin
1 red chile, seeded and finely chopped
¼ cup finely chopped fresh cilantro
¼ cup finely chopped fresh oregano
¼ cup finely chopped fresh mint
juice of ½ lemon
6 tablespoons olive oil

For the dukkah:
¼ cup unsalted pistachios
¼ cup peeled hazelnuts
¼ cup sesame seeds
2 tablespoons coriander seeds
2 tablespoons cumin seeds
2 teaspoons black peppercorns
2 teaspoons sumac
2 teaspoons sea salt

You will need eight 8in wooden skewers or two large metal skewers.

Preheat a grill pan or outdoor grill. Cut the ends off the eggplants, cut in half lengthwise, then cut each half in half again widthwise. Drizzle with olive oil, sprinkle with sea salt, and cook on each side until tender.

While the eggplant is cooking, prepare the marinade. Mix all the ingredients together and season with salt and pepper. Once the eggplants are tender, place in the marinade and toss to coat. Let marinate for at least 2 hours, preferably overnight in the fridge if you have the time, allowing them to return to room temperature before serving.

To make the dukkah, roast the nuts in a dry frying pan or hot oven and set aside to cool. (You could use pre-roasted nuts if you like.) Separately, dry-roast the seeds and peppercorns. Place the nuts, seeds, sumac, and salt in a blender or mortar and pestle and pulse/pound to a coarse bread crumb texture. Set aside. (You can make the dukkah up to 2 weeks in advance, storing it in an airtight container until required.)

Meanwhile, prepare the tahini sauce according to the instructions on page 160.

To assemble, skewer the eggplant pieces lengthwise onto the wooden skewers. If making to share, skewer widthwise onto two metal skewers (the double skewer will prevent the eggplants from spinning around). Pack the wedges closely together.

Sprinkle the dukkah over a plate, drizzle the skewers with a little tahini sauce, and roll in the dukkah to coat. You can serve the souvlaki at room temperature, but if you prefer to eat them warm, reheat the eggplant gently in the oven before drizzling with tahini and dukkah.

Any leftover dukkah is great sprinkled over smashed avocado or soft-boiled eggs.

WILD GREENS, MACARONI AND CHEESE

Spanakopita meets macaroni and cheese. Take advantage of nettles when in season, and purchase at the farmers' market or forage for the younger leaves that grow at the top of each spear. You could turn this dish into a delicious pie by sandwiching between two layers of filo dough (each being five layers thick and brushed with melted butter). Score the top and brush with melted butter, splash with water, and bake in the oven at 350°F for about 45 minutes until golden.

Serves 4–6

sea salt and freshly ground black pepper
1lb 10oz assorted wild greens, such as nettle tops, sorrel, or spinach and chard, coarse stems removed and roughly chopped
9oz macaroni noodles
5 tablespoons butter, plus extra for greasing
⅓ cup all-purpose flour
3¾ cups whole milk
1 teaspoon ground cinnamon
a pinch of freshly grated nutmeg
2 teaspoons Dijon mustard
3 cups mix of grated Kefalotyri or Pecorino and Cheddar, Gruyère, or Graviera *
8 scallions, finely sliced
¼ cup finely chopped fresh dill
⅓ cup fresh bread crumbs
⅔ cup crumbled feta

* Graviera is a Gruyère-style cheese made in Greece.

Preheat the oven to 350°F.

Bring a large saucepan of salted water to a boil, add the greens, and blanch for 1 minute. Remove and plunge into ice-cold water. Squeeze the excess water from the greens and set aside.

Cook the macaroni in the "greens" water for 3 minutes less than stated on the package. Drain and cool under running water to keep the pasta from cooking any further.

Meanwhile, melt 3½ tablespoons of the butter in a saucepan over medium heat, add the flour, and cook, stirring constantly, for a minute or two until the mixture is golden and grainy. Gradually whisk in the milk and cook until the sauce thickens and coats the back of a spoon (about 5 minutes). Remove the pan from the heat, add the cinnamon, nutmeg, mustard, and grated cheeses, and set aside.

Melt the remaining butter in a small pan, add the scallions, and cook until softened. Add the greens and cook for another 3 minutes, then combine with the sauce along with the dill and cooked macaroni. Season with salt and pepper to taste.

Pour into a greased, 2-quart baking dish and sprinkle the surface with bread crumbs and feta. Bake until golden and bubbling, about 25 minutes. Let rest for 5 minutes before serving.

Variations: To vary the filling, soften some sliced leeks or fennel with the scallions. For a richer sauce, you could add 2 beaten egg yolks or replace half of the milk with unsweetened condensed milk! If you prefer a non-vegetarian variety, pan-fry some sliced loukaniko or Italian fennel seed sausages and add to the macaroni and cheese.

PUMPKIN "SNAIL" PIES

These spicy, warming autumnal pies (called "snail" because of their shape, not their content!) are usually made with rice or bulgur wheat in Greece, but I'm making mine with chickpeas instead. I like to use the smaller, green-skinned or Japanese pumpkins as they're less watery than the orange-skinned ones, but if you can't find them, use butternut squash or kabocha instead. The pies taste great with Pomegranate Mint Yogurt (see below).

Variation: Add some cheese, such as 7oz crumbled feta or grated Kefalotyri, to the pie mixture.

POMEGRANATE MINT YOGURT

⅔ cup Greek yogurt
seeds from ½ pomegranate
1 green chile, finely chopped
1 tablespoon finely chopped
  mint leaves
a pinch of ground cumin
a pinch of sugar
1 tablespoon lime juice
sea salt

Mix the ingredients in a bowl, season with a little sea salt and refrigerate before serving.

Serves 4

1 teaspoon cumin seeds
1 teaspoon coriander seeds
½ teaspoon ground cinnamon
1 teaspoon ground cumin
1 teaspoon sweet paprika
sea salt and freshly ground black pepper
6 tablespoons olive oil
1¼lb green pumpkin or butternut squash, peeled
  and cut into ¾in chunks
2 large shallots, finely chopped
2 garlic cloves, finely chopped
⅔ cup whole blanched almonds, roughly chopped
½ cup cooked chickpeas, drained
⅓ cup raisins, soaked in warm water for 10 minutes
2 tablespoons lemon juice
½ bunch of fresh cilantro, chopped
8 sheets of filo dough
7 tablespoons unsalted butter, melted
1 free-range egg, beaten
3 tablespoons sesame seeds
¼ cup honey
pomegranate seeds and shredded mint leaves, to serve

Preheat the oven to 375°F. Dry-fry the cumin and coriander seeds in a small pan over medium heat. Grind in a mortar and pestle and add the remaining spices, a pinch of salt, and half the olive oil. Place the pumpkin or squash in a roasting pan and toss with the spiced oil mixture. Roast until tender, about 25 minutes.

Meanwhile, heat the remaining oil in a large saucepan over medium heat, add the shallots, and cook until they start to caramelize, about 6 minutes. Add the garlic and almonds and cook for 3 minutes, stirring frequently. Remove from the heat. Add the chickpeas, drained raisins, and pumpkin or squash and coarsely mash. Add the lemon juice and cilantro and season to taste.

Lay a sheet of filo on a clean work surface, brush with melted butter, and top with another layer. Spoon a quarter of the pumpkin filling along the longest side, leaving a ¾in gap at each end; fold in the sides, then loosely roll up and twist into a coil. Place on a baking sheet lined with parchment and repeat with the remaining dough and filling. Brush the tops with beaten egg, scatter with sesame seeds, and bake until golden, about 15–20 minutes. Drizzle with honey and serve hot or at room temperature, sprinkled with pomegranate seeds and shredded mint.

PAN-FRIED SEA BASS WITH BEET COUSCOUS, SPICED SEEDS, AND YOGURT SAUCE

"It's all Greek to me!" Well I guess you could say that about this recipe—Greeks love to use beets and here I've combined them with fresh herbs, dill, mint and parsley in particular. Dill cucumbers and capers add acidity and sharpness and, well, the ginger's just me being me!

You can make the couscous, spiced seeds, and yogurt ahead of time and assemble when you're ready to cook the fish.

Serves 4

For the beet couscous:
5½oz raw beets
½ cup cooked Puy, green, or beluga lentils
1 large shallot, finely chopped
1¾ tablespoons fresh ginger, finely grated
½ cup dill cucumbers or dill gherkins, finely diced
2 tablespoons capers, rinsed, roughly chopped
¾ cup fresh dill, finely chopped
¾ cup finely chopped fresh flat-leaf parsley
¾ cup finely chopped fresh mint
2 tablespoons Cabernet Sauvignon vinegar
2 tablespoons olive oil
sea salt and freshly ground black pepper

For the spiced seeds:
¼ cup sunflower seeds
¼ cup pumpkin seeds
1 teaspoon ground cumin
a pinch of cayenne pepper
2 tablespoons olive oil

For the yogurt sauce:
1 garlic clove, crushed
1 teaspoon sea salt
1 tablespoon tahini
a pinch of ground cumin
1 tablespoon lemon juice
¾ cup Greek yogurt

4 sea bass fillets, skin on and pin-boned
a glug of olive oil
a handful of pea shoots, to serve

Preheat the oven to 350°F.

Trim the ends off the beets, peel, and cut into small pieces. Place half in a food processor and pulse until the beets resemble couscous; transfer to a bowl and repeat with the remaining half.

Add the lentils, shallot, ginger, dill cucumber, capers, and herbs to the bowl. Dress with the vinegar and oil, then season with salt and pepper. Refrigerate until required.

For the spiced seeds, place the seeds and spices in a bowl. Add a generous pinch of sea salt and the oil, toss together, then spread on a baking sheet and roast for about 5–8 minutes until golden. Cool, then stir into the beet couscous just before serving.

Meanwhile, prepare the yogurt sauce: crush the garlic with sea salt, put in a bowl, and add the tahini and 1 tablespoon water. Mix well before adding the remaining ingredients. Refrigerate until required.

When everything's ready, pan-fry the sea bass. Place a large, nonstick frying pan over medium-high heat. Lightly score the skin of each (this will keep the fish flat while cooking so you'll get a nice crisp, even surface), turn over, and season with sea salt and black pepper. Add a dash of olive oil to the pan along with a little sea salt, then carefully add the bass skin-side down. Turn the heat to medium, press the fish down, and leave it to cook for about 4 minutes until the skin becomes crisp and golden. (Don't be tempted to turn it over beforehand.) Once crisp, turn over, reduce the heat a little, and cook for another 2 minutes.

To serve, smear a layer of the yogurt sauce on each plate, top with beet couscous, followed by the bass, skin-side up. Scatter with pea shoots, drizzle with a little olive oil, and serve immediately.

WHOLE BAKED SNAPPER

There's no better fish to cook on the bone than a meaty snapper. Stuffed and served whole, it will not only impress your guests with its appearance, but also its flavor; plus it's quick and easy to prepare! Replace salt with Lemon Oregano Salt (page 161) if you have some. Accompany with Stifado Fondant Potatoes (page 141) or some crusty bread and wilted greens/green salad.

Variations: Lay the fish on some finely sliced potatoes and fennel, season with sea salt, and drizzle with lemon juice and olive oil. Add ½ cup white wine and cook as directed.

Serves 4

1 x 3¼–4½lb snapper or 2 x 1lb 10oz snapper, gutted and cleaned
2 garlic cloves, finely chopped
8 anchovies, finely chopped
1½ cups Kalamata olives, pitted and coarsely chopped
½ cup coarsely chopped fresh flat-leaf parsley
½ cup olive oil
sea salt
1 lemon, thinly sliced
10½oz vine-ripened cherry tomatoes
6 sprigs of oregano
4 sprigs of thyme
extra-virgin olive oil, to drizzle

To serve:
a small handful of torn fresh herbs, such as dill, chives, or flat-leaf parsley
caperberries or caper leaves (optional)

Rinse the fish and pat dry. Preheat the oven to 375°F.

Mix together the garlic, anchovies, olives, parsley, and a little of the olive oil (about 2 tablespoons) to bind. Cut three incisions in each side of the fish and stuff with the anchovy-olive mixture. Season the cavity with sea salt and fill with lemon slices.

Place the cherry tomatoes, oregano, and thyme sprigs in an ovenproof dish large enough to hold the fish. Drizzle with the remaining olive oil and season with salt, place the snapper on top, and drizzle the skin with the remaining oil and a little more salt. Bake for about 25 minutes for smaller fish or up to 35 minutes for large fish—or until the flesh is opaque and offers no resistance when pierced with a toothpick.

When the snapper is cooked, serve on a platter, family-style, with the pan juices, a drizzle of extra-virgin olive oil, and a scattering of herbs and caperberries or leaves, if using.

MASTIC-CRUMBED RED SNAPPER WITH ORANGE, FENNEL, AND ENDIVE SALAD

Mastic is commonly used to make gum and is found in sweet dishes such as ice cream, Turkish delight, breads, and pastries. The Arabs used to combine mastic with coriander. In this recipe I use it with cumin and cinnamon.

Mastic is the resin of the evergreen mastic tree (Pistacia lentiscus), which grows throughout the Mediterranean, though it can only be harvested on the Greek island of Chios (where it has a PDO) due to its microclimate. The resin "weeps" out when the tree is scored and forms "tears" as it dries and hardens in the sun. Mastic is sold in crystal or liquid form and is "resiny" in flavor, with a unique aroma of pine trees, which always strikes me as odd as it's a member of the pistachio family! Most Greek, Turkish, and Arabic supermarkets will stock it, but you can buy it online through international grocery stores or try amazon.com. Mastic is extremely powerful, so you only need a small amount. Always grind the crystals with the addition of salt or sugar in a mortar and pestle or you'll end up with a gummy mess!

Variations: If you're not a fan of red snapper, use cod, bream, or bass fillets. As for the salad, you could add a little chopped cilantro or some shiso cress if available. Or omit the nigella seeds and replace with some finely chopped red onion.

Serves 4

4–5 small mastic crystals
1 tablespoon sea salt
½ cup instant polenta
2 teaspoons ground coriander
1 teaspoon ground cumin
1 teaspoon ground cinnamon
4 large or 8 small red snapper fillets, skin on, pin-boned
a glug of olive oil

For the salad:
3 small oranges
1 small bulb of fennel
1 head of endive, red or white
12 Kalamata olives, pitted and roughly chopped
½ cup olive oil
2 tablespoons white wine vinegar
a pinch of onion (nigella) seeds
16 mint leaves, torn

Pound the mastic with the salt in a mortar and pestle until powdered. Then mix with the polenta and spices in a shallow container. Set aside.

To make the salad, cut the ends off two of the oranges, then cut away the peel. Cut the oranges into ¼in-thick slices, removing any seeds, and reserve any juice for dressing. Halve the fennel lengthwise, discarding the tough outer layer, and core and thinly slice widthwise on a mandolin, or use a peeler. Halve the endive lengthwise and thinly slice.

Place some orange slices on a plate, top with alternate layers of fennel and endive, and scatter with the olives. Squeeze juice from the remaining orange and measure ¼ cup. Whisk this together with the oil and vinegar and drizzle over the salad, then scatter with onion seeds and torn mint leaves.

Brush the snapper flesh with olive oil and dredge in the polenta mixture to coat. Heat a little oil in a large nonstick frying pan over medium heat. Pan-fry the snapper, polenta-side down, for 2 minutes until golden; carefully turn over and cook for another minute or two or until the snapper is just cooked through and offers no resistance when pierced with a toothpick. Serve immediately, with the salad.

PAN-FRIED BREAM WITH POURGOURI, LENTILS, CHERRIES, AND MINT

Sea bream has a flaky texture and is a good choice for this recipe as the flavor is subtle but still tastes of the sea, but you could substitute the more readily available sea bass. You could serve this with wilted greens or some Greek yogurt, or omit the bream altogether and serve the pourgouri alone or with some Chile-Roasted Feta (page 30). The lentils are also delicious alongside Pickled Chicken (page 54).

Serves 4

¼ cup olive oil, plus extra for cooking
2 large onions, halved and thinly sliced
sea salt and freshly ground black pepper
½ cup brown lentils, rinsed
2 teaspoons ground cinnamon
2 cups water
¾ cup coarse pourgouri/bulgur wheat
4 sea bream fillets, skin on, pin-boned
1 cup black cherries, pitted and coarsely chopped
½ cup pine nuts or almonds, roasted or fried in a little olive oil
½ cup finely chopped fresh mint
2 tablespoons lemon juice
extra-virgin olive oil, for drizzling

Heat the olive oil in a large pan. Add the onions and a pinch of sea salt and cook over medium-low heat until caramelized. Don't rush this, it will take around 30 minutes; you'll need to stir them frequently, so they don't stick.

Meanwhile, put the lentils in a saucepan, cover with cold water, and bring to a boil. Simmer until partially cooked, about 10–15 minutes, but keep an eye on them. Drain and set aside.

Add the cinnamon to the caramelized onions and cook for 1 minute. Add the water and bring to a boil. Add the pourgouri/bulgur wheat and the drained lentils, reduce the heat to low, cover, and cook until the liquid has been absorbed and the pourgouri and lentils are cooked through but remain a little al dente (about 15–20 minutes). Remove from the heat and pour onto a baking sheet; cover with a kitchen towel while you cook the fish.

Heat a little oil in two nonstick frying pans or one large one over medium heat. Lightly score the skin of each fillet and place, skin-side down, in the hot pan(s). Cook for 2–3 minutes until the skin is crisp. Season with sea salt then carefully turn the fish over and cook for another 1–2 minutes. Remove the pan from the heat.

Stir the cherries, nuts, and mint through the lentil mixture, drizzle with lemon juice and extra-virgin olive oil, and season with salt and pepper. Serve alongside the pan-fried bream.

HOW TO PREPARE
AN OCTOPUS

To prepare an octopus, slice right below the octopus' eyes to separate the head from the tentacles. Remove the ink sac and innards from the head and discard (at this point you may get covered in black ink!). Using your thumbs, push the black beak (its mouth) out from the center of the tentacles and discard. Rinse the octopus (and your hands!) well under running water, making sure you clean the tentacles and head pouch thoroughly. The octopus is now ready to rock!

SLOW-BRAISED OCTOPUS WITH CHERRY TOMATO SAUCE

A lot of people are squeamish about cooking or eating octopus until they try it and realize how incredibly tasty and meltingly tender it is. You can always ask your fishmonger to clean the octopus if you don't want to do it yourself. The fishmonger will normally have tenderized the octopus for you too, so don't worry about that. If you've ever seen Greek fishermen thrashing an octopus against the rocks, it's not because they're having a bad day; they're just tenderizing it! This dish is best served with Kalamata Olive Gnocchi (page 83) or Feta Polenta (page 141).

Serves 4

For the octopus:
1 medium octopus, about 2¼lb, cleaned and prepared (page 78)
2 teaspoons fennel seeds
a pinch of dried red pepper flakes

For the tomato sauce:
2 tablespoons olive oil
2 garlic cloves, finely chopped
2 teaspoons fennel seeds
a pinch of dried red pepper flakes
2 tablespoons tomato paste
12oz cherry tomatoes
a pinch of sea salt and sugar
1 cup crumbled feta or grated Kefalotyri (optional)

Kalamata Olive Gnocchi or Feta Polenta, to serve

Preheat the oven to 300°F.

Select a roasting pan or Dutch oven in which the octopus will fit snugly. Place the prepared octopus in it and scatter with the fennel seeds and pepper flakes. Cover with foil and cook in the oven for about 2 hours, until the octopus is tender when pierced with the tip of a knife. Avoid overcooking—this can make the flesh tough.

Remove the octopus and set aside to cool. Pass the cooking liquid through a fine sieve and reserve. Slice the cooled tentacles and head into 1¼in pieces and set aside while you make the tomato sauce.

Heat the olive oil in a large, nonstick frying pan over low heat, then add the garlic, fennel seeds, and pepper flakes and cook for about 1 minute, until infused. Add the tomato paste and cook over medium heat for 1 minute, stirring continuously and being careful not to burn the garlic. Add the cherry tomatoes, a pinch of sea salt and sugar, and simmer over low heat for 5 minutes.

Add the octopus and its reserved cooking liquid. Simmer for another 5–10 minutes until reduced. Serve tossed with Kalamata Olive Gnocchi or Feta Polenta, and sprinkle with cheese, if using.

KALAMATA OLIVE GNOCCHI

My editor, Sophie, asked me to write about how I came up with this dish. I think I need a book twice this length to explain all the things that go on in my head when I come up with ideas! No, gnocchi is not Greek, but while I was making it one day I thought about how good it would be with some salty olives mixed through it. They'd also add color, although I was concerned they'd look like Garibaldi (dead fly) biscuits! Mixed with a rich tomato sauce, they're far more attractive, adding a comforting balance and depth. I'd cooked octopus for another dish that day, but as it came out of the oven I suddenly had this urge to try it with the sauce and gnocchi, three comfort foods together. And that's how the dish was born, out of curiosity. It's like fish and chips redefined, with a hint of Greek.

Serve with Slow-braised Octopus with Cherry Tomato Sauce (page 80), or simply tossed with grated Kefalotyri or feta cheese… salted anchovies… fresh tomatoes… basil… lamb… sardines … the world's your oyster!

Serves 4

2¼lb large, floury potatoes, such as Russets or Yukon Golds
sea salt and freshly ground black pepper
1⅓–1⅔ cups all-purpose flour, plus extra for dusting
⅓ cup pitted black Kalamata olives, roughly chopped
a pinch of grated nutmeg
1 free-range egg, lightly beaten
extra-virgin olive oil, for drizzling

Preheat the oven to 400°F.

Place the potatoes on a nonstick baking sheet and cook in the oven until tender, 1–2 hours, depending on their size. While they're still hot, halve and scoop out the flesh using a spoon. Pass through a fine sieve or potato ricer into a bowl.

Fill a large saucepan with salted water and bring to a boil while you prepare the gnocchi.

Place the potatoes on a clean work surface dusted with flour. Mix with the olives, salt, pepper, nutmeg, and two-thirds of the flour and lightly knead together. Make a well in the center, pour in the egg, and gradually work into the potato; use your hands to form a smooth, soft dough, adding more flour if necessary. Be careful not to overwork the dough.

I always like to test the dough by cooking a small piece in the boiling water. Cook until the gnocchi floats; if it falls apart, add a little more flour to the dough. Taste for seasoning and adjust as necessary.

Cut the dough into four, then roll each on a lightly floured surface into ¾in-diameter sausages and cut into 1¼in pieces. Place on a baking sheet lined with parchment paper and sprinkle lightly with flour. You can make the gnocchi ahead of time and refrigerate until required.

Cook the gnocchi in batches in the boiling water until they float to the surface (1–2 minutes). Remove with a slotted spoon or sieve and place in a warmed serving dish. Drizzle with olive oil and toss with the sauce of your choice. Serve immediately.

GREEK-STYLE PAELLA

This is my version of a favorite Spanish classic. Although saffron is grown in northern Greece, it's not widely used in Greek cooking generally, other than for flavoring cakes and cookies. Loukaniko is a fennel seed and orange flavored sausage. Italian fennel seed sausages are good alternatives. You could also use soutzouki (see page 47), or omit the sausage altogether. Chorizo would also work well if you can't find any Greek/fennel sausages.

Variation: Omit the sausage and add some monkfish, cod, or snapper instead—you'll need about 7oz net weight. Cut the fish into even-sized chunks and pan-fry it before you do the onions. Set aside and add to the rice with the mussels and shrimp.

Serves 4–6 (4 generously!)

½ cup olive oil
2 loukaniko, casing removed, cut into ¾in pieces
1 small onion, finely diced
½ fennel bulb, finely diced
3 garlic cloves, finely chopped
1½ teaspoons dried oregano
1 teaspoon paprika, or sweet smoked paprika
½ cup ouzo or dry white wine
1 x 10½oz can crushed tomatoes
sea salt and freshly ground black pepper
8oz calamari, cleaned and sliced into rings
a pinch of saffron, soaked in 1 tablespoon hot water
1½ cups short-grain rice, such as Calasparra
   (Spanish paella rice) or risotto rice
3¼ cups hot chicken or fish stock
8 raw jumbo shrimp
8oz mussels, cleaned
¾ cup peas, fresh or frozen
¾ cup feta, cubed
½ cup roughly chopped fresh dill
1 lemon, cut into wedges, to serve

You'll need a very large frying or paella pan (about 15in in diameter) to make this.

Heat a little of the olive oil in the pan, add the sausage, and sauté over medium heat until colored on each side (about 1 minute), then remove and set aside. Heat the remaining oil and add the onion, fennel, and garlic and cook until softened; stir in the oregano and paprika and cook for 1 minute more. Add the ouzo or wine and tomatoes, bring to a boil, then simmer for 10 minutes. Season with salt and pepper.

Stir in the calamari, saffron and soaking water, rice, and 2½ cups of the hot stock and arrange the rice so that it forms an even layer. Turn up the heat, bring the liquid to a boil, and cook, uncovered, over high heat for 10 minutes. Don't be tempted to stir! You want the rice to cook in its even layer. (If you've bought shrimp with shells on, peel them and add to the stock while it's warming to enhance the flavor.)

Arrange the sausage, shrimp, mussels, and peas on the surface, pushing them into the rice a little, and top with the feta cheese. Reduce the heat to low and cover with foil and cook for 5 minutes. Check the rice and, if it looks very dry, add a little more of the hot stock, but bear in mind that the paella shouldn't be soupy! Re-cover with foil and cook for another 3 minutes.

Take off the heat, loosen the foil, and let rest for 5 minutes. Sprinkle with dill and serve in the pan, with lemon wedges.

ROAST SPATCHCOCK CHICKEN WITH POTATOES, LEMON, WILD GREENS, AND CAPERS

This is a Greek classic with a small twist: tender, lemon-roasted chicken and deliciously soft roast potatoes that soak up the pan juices like little sponges! If time permits, I'd urge you to brine your chicken first (page 88).

Serves 2–4, depending on hunger!

1 x 3–3¼lb free-range chicken
3 garlic cloves
sea salt and freshly ground black pepper
1 tablespoon dried oregano
1 bay leaf, chopped
2 tablespoons olive oil
juice of 2 lemons
2lb potatoes, peeled, cut in half lengthwise, and then quartered
¾ cup chicken stock or water
2 tablespoons capers, rinsed
9oz mixed greens, such as spinach, chard, dandelion, arugula, or Pickled Caper Leaves (page 153), if you have them

Variation: You may also like to scatter with a little crumbled feta or replace the capers with olives.

You will need a good pair of kitchen scissors.

Preheat the oven to 350°F. First you need to spatchcock the chicken—it's easy, I promise! Remove the wing tips from the chicken. Place the chicken on a cutting board, breast-side down, and cut along either side of the backbone to remove (you can freeze this along with the wing tips and use for stock). Turn the chicken over and then, using the palm of your hand, press down on the chicken to make it flat and until you hear it crack.

Place the garlic in a mortar and pestle with a good pinch of sea salt and crush to a paste; add the oregano, bay leaf, olive oil, and half of the lemon juice and mix.

Massage most of the mixture over the breast side of the chicken, getting right into the leg joints, then rub a little on the other side. (If you have time, and haven't brined your chicken, pop it in the fridge and let it marinate for an hour. Make sure you remove it from the fridge half an hour before cooking, though.)

Put the potatoes in a roasting pan, sprinkle with sea salt, and drizzle with olive oil and the remaining lemon juice. Place the chicken on top, breast-side up, and pour the stock or water around the edges.

Place in the oven and cook for 45–50 minutes, basting occasionally, or until the skin is golden brown and the juices run clear when the thickest part of the chicken is pierced with a knife. Transfer the chicken to a warm plate, cover with foil, and let rest.

Baste the potatoes and return to the top part of the oven for another 10 minutes, by which time they will be meltingly tender, golden, and will have soaked up some of the delicious pan juices. Transfer the potatoes to a warm platter and place the roasting pan on the stove over medium heat. Add the capers and greens and toss to wilt in the pan juices (if you're using caper leaves, there's no need to wilt). Adjust the seasoning and spoon over the potatoes.

Cut the chicken into two or four depending on hunger. Place on top of the potatoes and serve.

HOW TO BRINE A CHICKEN

To brine or not to brine?

In a two-sentence nut-shell, brining adds extra moisture and flavor to meat through osmosis and "protein modification," i.e. the meat absorbs the water and the proteins break down, resulting in a far juicer piece of meat, with added flavor. Sugar, herbs, and spices all add additional levels of flavor.

Once you've brined, you'll never look back!

Things to bear in mind:

– Brined meat tends to cook quicker than a non-brined piece, since the permeated water acts as a conductor of heat.

– Don't overseason brined meat when cooking; season at a point when you can taste it.

– Rinse the brined meat before cooking and pat dry.

– Brining times depend on the size of the meat and its thickness.

– Don't substitute the sea salt with another salt. Not all salts are the same: for example 40g of fine sea salt is the equivalent to 100g of table salt and 70g of coarse sea salt.

– Experiment by replacing the water with tea, cider, or beer, or a percentage of the water with bourbon, apple juice, or lemon juice. The sugar can be replaced with honey, maple syrup, or molasses.

– Mix and match with herbs and spices, bearing in mind that whatever flavor you choose determines the flavor your meat assumes.

– My friend Marc Frederick (Master charcutier and butcher) recommends a standard formula using a 3–5% salt solution i.e. 30g or 50g of salt per quart of water. He also advises using a 5-quart plastic bucket if possible (depends on your fridge space), adding 1 quart of brine at a time until the meat is completely covered. Using a narrow container means you will need less brine to cover the meat. A ziplock/freezer bag also works a treat when placed within a bucket/large jug.

– Never use curing salts as they'll turn the meat and bones pink, which will give the impression the meat is undercooked.

BASIC BRINE

Use this brine for Spatchcock Chicken (page 86)

60g fine sea salt *
¼ cup superfine sugar

Combine the salt and sugar in a saucepan with 2 cups cold water and stir over medium heat until the sugar and salt dissolve. Remove from the heat and add another 1½ quarts of cold water. Let cool completely before transferring to a non-reactive container or Ziplock bag big enough to submerge the chicken in the brine. Add the spatchcocked chicken and refrigerate overnight or for 6–10 hours.

Rinse under running water and proceed with the recipe on page 86.

HOW TO POACH A CHICKEN

1 x 4½lb free-range chicken, at room temperature
a glug of olive oil
1 cup dry white wine
2 celery ribs, roughly chopped
1 onion, roughly chopped
1 carrot, peeled and roughly chopped
2 garlic cloves
2 bay leaves
a few fresh parsley stems
6 thyme sprigs
10 whole black peppercorns

Remove any giblets from your chicken and trim off any excess fat.

Heat the oil in a stockpot large enough to hold the chicken and enough water to cover. Once the oil is hot, sear the chicken until golden on each side, then remove from the pan. Add the white wine, turn up the heat, and reduce until almost evaporated.

Add the celery, onion, carrot, garlic, herbs, and peppercorns to the pot, along with the chicken, and pour in enough cold water to cover the chicken by an inch or two. Place over medium-high heat and bring almost to a boil, then reduce the heat so the water is simmering gently.

Cook for 1½ hours, skimming regularly and adding more water if necessary to keep the chicken covered. Remove from the heat, cover, and let stand for an hour. The chicken will continue to cook gently.

Lift the chicken from the liquid, pull the meat from the bones, and discard the bones. Strain the liquid through a fine sieve, discard the vegetables etc., skim the fat, and reserve the broth. If you're making in advance, refrigerate the shredded chicken in some of the cooled cooking broth (which will help keep it moist).

You're now ready to rock and roll with the soup recipe on page 91.

Variation: For a simpler version, place the chicken in a pot with the aromatics (the other ingredients), excluding the wine, cover with water, and proceed as above.

CHICKEN SOUP WITH ORZO, SHREDDED GRAPE LEAVES, TOMATOES, LEMON, AND HERBS

There's nothing more comforting than a bowl of chicken soup... I'd recommend you poach a whole chicken (see page 89) a day in advance. Or, if you have half a roast chicken leftover, strip the meat from it and make a stock from the roasted carcass: place the stripped carcass in a pot with ½ an onion, 2 cloves garlic, 1 rib celery, a bay leaf, and a carrot if you have one. Cover with cold water and place over low heat for 1 hour. Turn off heat and let cool before straining. Discard the carcass and aromatics, and your stock is ready!

I adore the flavor and smell of stuffed grape leaves. They bring back childhood memories of spending Sundays at my Aunty Stella's, and to this day I've never eaten a dolmades (stuffed grape leaves) as good as hers.

While writing this recipe I got to thinking that some soaked raisins and shaved Kefalotyri would be good to serve with this soup. I also tried it topped with a little crumbled feta, which was great. Next time I make it I'm going to add some peeled fava beans. Basically, go with whatever you think sounds good!

Any leftover meat from the poached chicken would be great in a whimsical Ouzo, Celeriac, and Fennel Remoulade sandwich (page 148).

Serves 4–6

2 tablespoons olive oil
1 onion, finely diced
2 garlic cloves, finely chopped
a pinch of ground allspice
1 teaspoon ground cinnamon
1 quart reserved chicken stock (from poaching, page 89)
¾ cup orzo
4 large, vine-ripened tomatoes, peeled and diced
8 grape leaves (fresh or pickled), trimmed of stem and shredded*
½ reserved chicken meat from poaching (page 89)
¼ cup finely chopped fresh mint
¼ cup finely chopped fresh dill
¼ cup finely chopped fresh flat-leaf parsley
2 tablespoons freshly squeezed lemon juice
sea salt and freshly ground black pepper
extra-virgin olive oil, to serve

* If using fresh grape leaves, blanch them in boiling salted water for about 2 minutes until they're no longer bright green; refresh under cold running water. If using pickled or jarred leaves, place in a colander and rinse well.

Heat the oil in a medium saucepan over medium heat, add the onion, and cook for 5–8 minutes until softened and transparent. Add the garlic, allspice, and cinnamon and cook for another minute, then add the chicken stock and bring almost to a boil. Add the orzo, tomatoes, grape leaves, and chicken then reduce the heat so the soup is simmering. Cook for approximately 8 minutes, or until the orzo is tender.

Add the fresh herbs and lemon juice and season with salt and pepper. Serve drizzled with extra-virgin olive oil.

FRIED BUTTERMILK CHICKEN

OK, don't be put off, but if you want to make an amazing-tasting piece of chicken you will need to give it some time! By that I mean that you need to start the recipe one or two days ahead by brining the chicken (page 88). It will make the world of difference; believe me, it's well worth the wait. My friend Elena tried this recipe and said, "Brining was a revelation to me, I've been won over!"

I like to serve the chicken with Tahini Sauce (page 160), smashed baby potatoes mixed with crème fraîche and mint, and a crisp iceberg salad with Ouzo Lemon Dressing (page 161).

Serves 2, or 3–4 if you're not greedy!

3lb free-range chicken, cut into 10 pieces (wings, thighs, drumsticks, and breast cut in two through the bone), or 3lb chicken thighs and drumsticks, skin and bone on
oil for frying, e.g. vegetable, canola, or peanut
lemon wedges, to serve

For the brine:
60–80g fine sea salt*
¼ cup superfine sugar
1 tablespoon black peppercorns
4 garlic cloves, bruised
12 oregano sprigs, roughly chopped
2 bay leaves
zest and juice of 2 lemons

For the coating:
1½ cups cornstarch
½ cup fine semolina
2 teaspoons dried oregano
1 tablespoon garlic powder
1½ teaspoons paprika
1 teaspoon ground cinnamon
a pinch of ground allspice
1 teaspoon ground cumin
½ teaspoon cayenne pepper
1 teaspoon sea salt
1 teaspoon freshly ground black pepper
¾ cup buttermilk
2 free-range eggs

Combine the salt and sugar in a large saucepan with 2 cups cold water. Stir over medium heat until the sugar and salt dissolve. Remove from the heat and add another 1.3 quarts cold water. Add the remaining brine ingredients and stir to combine. Let cool completely before transferring to a non-reactive container big enough to accommodate the chicken. Add the chicken pieces and refrigerate for 6–8 hours or overnight.

Drain the chicken, rinse under cold water, and pat dry thoroughly. If you have time, refrigerate the chicken, uncovered, for up to one day before you cook it, which helps the skin dry out—if you can wait that long!

Remove the chicken from the fridge and let it come up to room temperature. It's really important that you do this, so that the chicken will cook evenly.

Preheat the oven to 400°F. Combine the flour and semolina with the oregano, garlic powder, spices, and seasoning and divide between two bowls. Whisk the buttermilk with the eggs and place in a third bowl, set in between the flour bowls. Dip the chicken pieces into the flour, then the egg mixture, followed by the flour again.

Heat about ¾in oil in a large frying pan over medium heat. Once it's hot (325°F, which means that a cube of bread will brown in 30 seconds), add the chicken in batches of 3–4 pieces and cook until lightly golden. Transfer to a cooling rack placed over a baking sheet or to a baking sheet lined with parchment paper. Place in the oven for 25–30 minutes to finish cooking (the core temperature should be above 150°F). Let rest for 5 minutes, sprinkle with salt, and serve with lemon wedges.

Variations: I like to use cornstarch and semolina as I think it gives a crisper, lighter coating, but you can use all-purpose flour instead. You can, of course, vary the flour seasoning, too. Crushed, roasted fennel or celery seeds would make a great addition, or even some red pepper or aleppo pepper flakes.

* Don't substitute the sea salt with another salt—see page 88 for further details.

RABBIT BAKLAVA

I admit, this isn't the shortest of recipes, but it's one you can break down into stages over a period of days or even weeks by making the rabbit confit in advance. The onion and bean mixture can also be made ahead of time and then all you have to do is assemble when required. It's a recipe I had on one of my restaurant menus and I always promised that I'd share it with you one day!

You'll need to make the Rabbit Confit on page 58 for this recipe, but double the amounts—so use 4 rabbit legs, 2 tablespoons sea salt, 4 cloves garlic, 6 sprigs thyme, 2¼lb duck fat, and 2 cinnamon sticks.

This baklava is delicious served with a lemon-dressed Swiss chard salad and Parsnip Skordalia (page 131). Fava Bean and Mint Hummus (page 132), or Tahini Sauce (page 160) are also good accompaniments.

Serves 4–8

¼ cup olive oil
¼ cup duck fat from the confit (page 58)
4 Spanish onions, halved and finely sliced
2 garlic cloves, peeled and finely chopped
2 teaspoons ground cinnamon
a pinch of granulated sugar
¼ cup finely chopped fresh oregano
   (or 4 teaspoons dried)
2 x 14oz cans butter beans
sea salt and freshly ground black pepper
2 tablespoons lemon juice
9 sheets of filo dough
1 stick + 2 tablespoons melted butter
rabbit meat from 4 confit legs, shredded (page 58)
½ cup blanched almonds, blitzed to a coarse crumble
⅔ cup Greek or Medjool dates, pitted and
   finely sliced
1¾ cups feta cheese, crumbled
honey, to serve

Preheat the oven to 350°F.

Heat the olive oil and duck fat in a large, heavy-bottomed saucepan. Gently cook the onions over low heat until softened; this can take up to about 20 minutes. Add the garlic, cinnamon, and sugar and increase the heat a little; cook for about 5 minutes longer, until caramelized. Add the oregano and butter beans and warm through over low heat for another 5 minutes. (If you have a layer of jelly from the rabbit confit on page 58, add this to the beans now.)

Pulse the bean mixture using a hand blender or food processor to break the beans down a little so you have a kind of chunky hummus. Season with salt and pepper and stir in the lemon juice.

Unfold the dough and cut it in half or as needed to fit your baking sheet (I'd suggest using one that's about 8 x 12in). Keep the dough covered with a damp cloth to prevent it from drying out. Brush the baking sheet with melted butter and line the pan with a sheet of filo, brush with butter again, and repeat until you have a five-layer thickness, brushing the top layer with butter.

Spread half the onion-bean mixture over the pastry. Top with half the shredded rabbit meat followed by half the almonds, dates, and feta. Top with the remaining onion-bean mixture, rabbit, almonds, dates, and feta. Sandwich together 4 layers of filo with melted butter and place on top. Lightly score the surface, cutting into diamonds approximately 4 x 1½in, then brush with butter and splash the surface with a little water. Place on a baking sheet and cook for 35–45 minutes or until golden.

Let cool slightly before serving, drizzling the surface with a little honey.

WILD FENNEL AND HALLOUMI STUFFED RABBIT COOKED OVER OLIVE WOOD

I cooked this dish for my dad over the charcoal grill in his restaurant. Inspired by the distillation process and flavorings of ouzo (which I'd read about in the inflight magazine en route to Cyprus), I decided to apply some of the elements to rabbit, a sensational-tasting meat that's sadly often underused. The olive branches, which are presoaked in water, give a gentle aroma and flavor to the rabbit as it cooks, as do the fennel twigs. If you have the time, brine your rabbit before cooking as it will add an extra depth of flavor, tenderize, and also help prevent the meat from drying out during cooking.

Wild fennel is a favorite ingredient of mine. It grows dramatically tall and sprouts beautiful yellow blossoms which burst with flavor. When the flowers are fresh, they're full of sweet fennel pollen, but be warned: you need a lot of fresh flowers to gather a small amount of pollen, hence its high price. The dried flowers are full of aromatic fennel seeds and the woody, twig-like stems are a great way of infusing flavor into an ingredient.

Don't panic if you don't have olive wood or wild fennel, I've added alternatives! And if the thought of using a whole rabbit fills you with fear, use four hind legs instead. Try serving the rabbit family-style in a roasting pan, with Fava Bean Purée (page 137), Dino's Pickled Caper Leaves (page 153), or a combination of capers and wilted greens, and drizzled with Ouzo Lemon Dressing (page 161).

Serves 4

4½lb whole, oven-ready rabbit, head on or off

For the brine:
50g fine sea salt *
3½ tablespoons sugar
2 quarts plus 2 cups cold water
½ cup white wine vinegar
3 garlic cloves, bruised
2 teaspoons black peppercorns
10 oregano sprigs, roughly chopped
1 bay leaf
2 strips of lemon zest

* Don't substitute with another salt. Not all salts are the same; see page 88 for details.

Combine the salt and sugar in a pan with the 2 cups water and warm gently until the salt and sugar are dissolved. Remove the pan from the heat and whisk in the vinegar, garlic, peppercorns, herbs, lemon zest, and 2 quarts cold water. Let cool completely.

Place the rabbit in a non-reactive container or Ziplock bag and pour the cooled brine over to cover. If not using a bag, cover the rabbit with a piece of parchment paper with a weighted plate or dish on top to keep the rabbit submerged. Leave in a cool place, allowing 1 hour of brining per 1lb 2oz of rabbit (i.e. 4 hours for a 4½lb rabbit).

Remove from the brine, pat the rabbit dry and proceed with the recipe (see right). Discard the brine.

OLIVE WOOD AND FENNEL TWIG VERSION

4½lb rabbit, brined as on page 94
4 olive branches, soaked in water for 10 minutes
about 20 wild fennel twigs
¾ cup water
a good glug of olive oil
sea salt and freshly ground black pepper
4oz halloumi, thinly sliced
juice of ½ lemon
¼ cup ouzo
1 cup water or chicken stock

You will need a large roll of aluminum foil.

Preheat the oven to 325°F or light the outdoor grill.
Line a roasting pan (large enough to fit a wire rack
inside) with aluminum foil. Scatter the olive wood
across the bottom of the pan and top with a few of the
fennel twigs. Add the ¾ cup water and place a wire
rack on top. Lay a double sheet of foil big enough to
hold the rabbit on the rack and place the rabbit on
the foil.

Drizzle the cavity of the rabbit with olive oil, season
with salt and pepper (not too much if you've brined the
rabbit), and fill with the halloumi slices and the rest of
the fennel twigs, using a few of the more pliable ones
to sew the cavity together. Fold all four foil edges up to
form a little wall around the rabbit. Drizzle with olive
oil, the lemon juice, ouzo, and 1 cup water or stock.
Cover the whole pan loosely with foil and carefully
place in the oven. Cook for about 1½–2 hours until
tender, basting the rabbit every half an hour.

If cooking over a charcoal grill, place the rabbit parcel
on the barbecue and cover with the barbecue lid or an
upturned roasting pan.

Remove the rabbit and rest, covered with foil, for 10
minutes. Pour the cooking liquid into a small saucepan
and reduce by a third for a thicker sauce. Slice the
rabbit in two across the saddle, remove the legs, spoon
with the cooking juices, and serve immediately.

FENNEL SEED & ROSEMARY VERSION (IF YOU DON'T HAVE OLIVE WOOD)

Substitute the olive branches and wild fennel twigs
for 2 tablespoons fennel seeds and 3 sprigs rosemary.
Follow the recipe as for the olive wood version,
scattering half the fennel seeds across the bottom of
the pan instead of olive wood, then filling the cavity
with the other half instead of fennel twigs. Sew the
cavity together with the rosemary sprigs instead of
fennel twigs, using the woody end to pierce the flesh.
Continue with the recipe as directed.

Variation: You could also fill the cavity of quails and
fish with these ingredients and cook over olive wood
for fantastic, flavorful results.

ROAST PARTRIDGE WITH HALLOUMI AND GRAPES

I saw a lot of partridges scurrying and waddling around the Cypriot mountains –they were the funniest things! It seemed only natural to combine them with ingredients from their habitat. Both grapes and walnuts are harvested around the time that the partridge season begins. Halloumi is used to keep the birds moist. Serve with the Cinnamon and Walnut Pourgouri on page 146, or a simple green salad dressed with walnut oil. If you want to add a touch of tradition when serving the game birds, lightly fry four slices of Greek bread in a little butter and olive oil and sit your partridge on top! You could also use quails for this recipe, but you'll need to reduce the cooking time considerably.

Serves 4

8 large fresh grape leaves, or pickled leaves if fresh unavailable
5½oz halloumi
4 plump partridges, oven ready
sea salt and freshly ground black pepper
8 thyme sprigs
8 oregano sprigs
8 slices thick-cut bacon
7 tablespoons unsalted butter
2 tablespoons grape jelly, or quince jelly or paste if unavailable, or fig jam!
¾ cup Mavrodaphne, Commandaria, or port
1¼ cups chicken stock
¾ cup green or black seedless grapes

Preheat the oven to 400°F.

Blanch the grape leaves in boiling salted water for 1 minute. Refresh in cold water, pat dry with paper towels, and trim off any stems. (If using pickled leaves, rinse well and pat dry with paper towels.)

Cut the halloumi into four and wrap each piece in a vine leaf. Season the partridges inside and out with salt and pepper. Place a halloumi parcel in each along with the thyme and oregano sprigs.

Place two bacon slices over each bird and top with a vine leaf. Tie the legs together with string to secure, place in a roasting pan, and dot with the butter. Roast for 15 minutes, then peel the vine leaf from the surface and discard. Baste the birds with the juices and return to the oven for another 10 minutes until the bacon is crisp and the partridges are cooked. Remove the birds and place on a plate, cover with foil, and rest for at least 10 minutes.

Put the roasting pan on the stove over medium heat, add the jelly, and let it melt into the juices. Add the wine to deglaze and reduce by half; add the stock, bring to a boil, and simmer for 5 minutes. Add the grapes and cook for another 2 minutes.

Remove the string from the partridges and serve, spooning the sauce over the top.

DUCK SHEPHERD'S PIE

There's nothing more comforting than shepherd's pie. Here it's been given a Greek twist. If you have the time, marinate the duck legs for 2–24 hours before using.

You could always purchase two whole ducks and butcher down, using the breasts for Cured Duck "Ham" (page 56) and the carcass for stock. Serve with wilted greens or a watercress salad.

Serves 4–6

4 duck legs
2 strips of orange zest
freshly squeezed juice of ½ orange
1 teaspoon ground cinnamon
a pinch of ground allspice
½ cup Mavrodaphne or port
¾ cup red wine
a glug of olive oil
1 onion, diced
1 carrot, diced
2 celery ribs, diced
2 garlic cloves, finely chopped
1 tablespoon tomato paste
1 tablespoon flour
3 teaspoons finely chopped fresh oregano
3 teaspoons finely chopped fresh thyme
1 bay leaf
3 cups duck or chicken stock
sea salt and freshly ground black pepper
1½ cups either crimini or shiitake
   mushrooms, sliced

For the mashed potato:
2¼lb red-skinned potatoes, peeled and diced into
   even-sized pieces
½ cup heavy cream
3 tablespoons butter
a pinch of nutmeg

Place the duck legs, orange zest and juice, spices, Mavrodaphne or port, and red wine in a non-reactive container. Cover and marinate in the fridge for 2 hours, or overnight if you have time. Remove from the fridge and bring up to room temperature before using.

Heat a little olive oil in a large saucepan. Pat the duck legs dry with paper towels and sear over medium heat until golden brown on each side. Remove the legs and drain away a little of the rendered fat before adding the onion. Caramelize for 5 minutes, then add the carrot, celery, and garlic and cook for 2 minutes more. Add the tomato paste and flour and cook, stirring continuously, for another 2 minutes.

Add the herbs and orange-and-wine marinade and bring to a boil. Cook for 5 minutes, skimming the surface to remove any impurities. Add the duck legs and stock, season, and bring to a simmer. Cover and cook for 1½–2 hours, or until the duck legs are tender.

While the duck is cooking, season and sauté the mushrooms in a little oil and set aside.

Meanwhile, cook the potatoes in boiling salted water or steam until tender, then drain and return to the heat for a minute or two to dry. Pass through a ricer or use a masher. Heat the cream and beat into the potatoes with the butter and nutmeg, and mix until smooth. Season with salt and pepper and set aside.

When the duck is cooked, remove it from the sauce and, once it's cool enough to touch, shred the meat from the bones, discarding the skin, fat, and bones.

Preheat the oven to 400°F.

Discard the bay leaf and orange peel from the sauce and skim the surface of fat. Reduce the sauce until it has thickened slightly; add the mushrooms and shredded duck and place in a heatproof dish or four individual ones. Top with the mashed potato and cook for about 20 minutes or until bubbling and golden brown. If you prefer a crisper top, brown under a broiler.

Variations: Cook the duck legs with some chopped quince or prunes or even a few pickled walnuts. For a different mash, you could try using two-thirds potato and one-third celeriac, or adding ½ cup Kefalotyri, Pecorino, or feta.

RARE ROAST LAMB WITH BROCCOLI, MINT, PINE NUT, AND RAISIN COUSCOUS

This is a striking recipe relatively easily achieved. Raw broccoli couscous is packed with flavor, a perfect accompaniment to rare roasted lamb, all brought together with a broccoli purée made from the stalks. The couscous can be made ahead of time, if need be.

Serves 4

For the marinade:
2 tablespoons olive oil
1 tablespoon lemon juice
a pinch of dried mint
sea salt and freshly ground black pepper

1lb lamb neck fillets, lamb shanks, or four lamb
   necks (average weight ¼lb each), trimmed
a drizzle of extra-virgin olive oil
pea shoots to garnish (optional)

For the broccoli couscous:
1 medium head of broccoli, florets only
3 tablespoons raisins, soaked in warm water
   until plump
a handful of toasted pine nuts
¾ cup finely chopped fresh mint
¾ cup finely chopped fresh flat-leaf parsley
juice of 1–2 lemons
½ cup olive oil

For the broccoli purée:
a glug of olive oil
1 large shallot, finely sliced
1 garlic clove, finely chopped
reserved broccoli stalks, finely sliced
1 potato, peeled and finely sliced
1½ cups chicken stock
1½ tablespoons raisins (golden if you have them),
   soaked in a little warm water until plump
½ cup finely chopped fresh flat-leaf parsley
½ cup finely chopped fresh mint
juice of 1 lemon

Preheat the oven to 400°F.

Prepare the marinade: Pour the olive oil, lemon juice, and mint in a non-reactive bowl, add salt and pepper and the lamb and mix well. Marinate for 20 minutes.

For the couscous, trim the stalks from the broccoli (set these aside for the purée). Place half the florets in a food processor and pulse until their texture resembles couscous. Pour into a large bowl and repeat with the remaining broccoli. Add the drained raisins, pine nuts, mint, and parsley. Season with sea salt, add the lemon juice and olive oil, stir, and serve. (If making ahead of time, dress with lemon juice and olive oil just before serving; refrigerate until required.)

To make the purée, heat the oil in a medium saucepan, add the shallot and garlic, and cook over medium heat until softened, about 5 minutes. Add the reserved broccoli stalks, potato, and stock, bring to a boil, then simmer until the broccoli and potato are tender and most of the stock has been absorbed, about 20 minutes. Pour into a blender, add the drained raisins, parsley, mint, and lemon juice, and process until smooth. Season with sea salt and pepper. Keep warm.

Heat a nonstick frying pan or grill pan over medium to high heat and sear the lamb on all sides until brown— about 5 minutes. Place the lamb on a roasting pan and put in the oven for just 5–8 minutes. Remove and rest for 5 minutes.

Spoon some of the warm purée onto plates, top with broccoli couscous and sliced lamb, drizzle with extra-virgin olive oil, and garnish with pea shoots.

LAMB, ORANGE, AND CHILE KEBABS

Lamb is usually associated with lemon in Greek cooking, but I thought it would make a change to use orange and chile instead to impart a great flavor and visual appeal to the lamb. Serve with a mint yogurt or tahini sauce, pita bread, salad, and pickles. You will need to start this the day before.

Variations: For alternative marinade flavors, add 6 sprigs of finely chopped oregano or 2 sprigs of stripped rosemary, and replace the orange peel with lemon.

Serves 4–6

2¼lb (net weight) trimmed boneless lamb shoulder
½ cup olive oil
4 garlic cloves, crushed with 1 tablespoon sea salt
2 bay leaves, finely chopped
2½ teaspoons ground cinnamon
1 teaspoon ground allspice
1 large orange
2 red chiles, halved lengthwise and seeded
sea salt and freshly ground black pepper
honey, to drizzle

You will need four 12in metal skewers or two double-pronged skewers.

Cut the lamb into roughly 2½in pieces and place in a non-reactive bowl. Add the oil, crushed garlic and salt, bay leaves, cinnamon, and allspice and toss evenly to coat.

Strip the zest from the orange using a vegetable peeler, cutting away any white pith. Add to the lamb, along with the chiles. Cut the orange in half and squeeze the juice over the lamb, and toss everything together. Cover and refrigerate overnight.

Remove the lamb from the fridge, season with salt and pepper, and mix well. Cut the orange peel and chiles into pieces. Thread a piece of lamb onto two skewers, leaving a ¾in distance between each skewer (two skewers will stop the meat from spinning), and follow with a piece of orange peel and a piece of chile. Repeat until all the lamb has been threaded onto the skewers. Let the lamb come up to room temperature before cooking.

Preheat a grill pan or outdoor grill to low heat and cook the lamb, turning occasionally, for about 30 minutes or until cooked to your liking. (You could, of course, sear the lamb on a grill pan or outdoor grill and finish in a preheated oven at 350°F for 15–20 minutes.) Set aside, drizzled with honey and covered with foil, to rest for 15 minutes before serving.

MARINATED LAMB WITH FETA CURD, PEAS, AND ARTICHOKES

This is spring on a plate! You might want to ask your butcher to butterfly a whole leg of lamb, which you can barbecue if you're cooking for 6 or more. This is a great way to use up the oil from a jar of artichokes, although of course you could use fresh ones, prepared and cooked yourself. Be sure to use artichokes marinated in olive rather than vegetable oil, otherwise they will taste gross!

If you're using a boneless leg of lamb, add extra marinade and cook over a hot grill for approximately 8–10 minutes on either side, then rest well. Serve family-style on a large plate.

Serves 4

14oz boneless leg of lamb
a drizzle of olive oil
sea salt and freshly ground black pepper
a pinch of dried oregano
¼ cup honey

For the feta curd:
⅔ cup feta, crumbled
2 tablespoons lemon juice
5 tablespoons artichoke oil (from the jar, see left)
freshly ground black pepper

For the peas:
1 cup fresh peas (podded weight)—you can use frozen
  petit pois if peas are out of season
1 large garlic clove, crushed
½ cup chopped fresh mint
½ cup chopped fresh dill
⅔ cup feta, crumbled
a little freshly grated lemon zest and 2 tablespoons juice
¼ cup olive or artichoke oil

To serve:
1 small jar of artichokes in olive oil, artichokes quartered
a handful of pea shoots
extra-virgin olive oil

Rub the lamb with a little oil, salt, pepper, and oregano. Let marinate for 30 minutes, or overnight in the fridge if you have time. Bring back to room temperature before cooking. Preheat a grill pan over medium heat. Sear the meat for 4–5 minutes on each side (or cook to your liking), then remove from the grill pan, drizzle with honey, and rest in a warm place.

Meanwhile make the curd. Blend the ⅔ cup feta, lemon juice, and oil in a blender until smooth. Season with pepper and set aside.

In batches, lightly crush the peas in a mortar and pestle and transfer to a bowl. Stir in the crushed garlic, mint, and dill, followed by the other ⅔ cup feta, lemon zest, juice, and oil. Season.

Smear the feta curd over your serving plates and spoon over some crushed peas. Slice the lamb and divide evenly between the plates, then top with artichoke quarters and sprinkle with pea shoots. Drizzle with olive oil and serve.

BRAISED LAMB WITH GREEN BEANS AND TOMATOES

I love this dish. It's one my mom used to make, using my dad's Greek-Cypriot method of braising meat in a rich, tomato sauce—such a delicious way to prepare lamb. The cooked lamb emerges full of flavor and melt-in-the-mouth tender, and the potatoes soak up all the wonderful cooking juices. It tastes even better the day after it's made. I use scrag end of lamb, or shoulder, which is a flavorful and economic cut from the neck that is so underused these days.

Serves 4

4 garlic cloves, finely chopped
2 teaspoons sea salt
zest of ½ lemon
2 tablespoons olive oil
2¼lb scrag end of lamb or lamb shoulder, on the bone
1 Spanish onion, finely chopped
1 celery rib, finely chopped
4 teaspoons tomato paste
6 tomatoes, peeled and roughly chopped, or 1 x 14oz can plum tomatoes, chopped
1 quart chicken stock
sea salt and freshly ground black pepper
1 fresh bay leaf
1 cinnamon stick
14oz medium potatoes, peeled and quartered
2 cups green beans or flat beans, sliced into 2½in pieces
¾ cup chopped fresh dill
¾ cup chopped fresh flat-leaf parsley

Crush 2 of the garlic cloves with the sea salt to form a paste. Mix with the lemon zest and half the olive oil, then rub all over the lamb. Let marinate for 1 hour or overnight in the fridge if you have time (be sure to bring the lamb back up to room temperature before cooking).

Heat the rest of the olive oil over medium heat in a pan large enough to hold the lamb and potatoes. Once hot, brown the lamb in batches and set aside. Add the onion, remaining garlic, and celery to the pan and cook until softened before adding the tomato paste. Cook for another minute, then add the tomatoes and chicken stock. Bring to a boil, season with salt and pepper, and add the bay leaf, cinnamon stick, and finally the lamb. Cover and simmer for 1¼ hours.

Add the potatoes and simmer for 20 minutes, uncovered. Add the string beans, dill, and half the parsley and simmer for another 15 minutes, until the beans and potatoes are tender. Skim the sauce of any fat and season to taste.

Serve in deep bowls, sprinkled with the remaining parsley.

SLOW-ROASTED PAPER-WRAPPED LEG OF LAMB

A simple, delicious recipe—and always a crowd-pleaser. Because the village baker's oven was always in use, people used to take their meat to be slow-roasted in the residual heat of the oven after the morning bake. Such a sense of community spirit! The lamb is gorgeous served with lemon-roasted potatoes or Gigantes Plaki (page 20), Lemon and Dill-Braised Fava Beans (page 135), Tomato and String Bean Baklava (page 64), or a green salad—the choice is endless. Or use it to make a good old-fashioned lamb sandwich—dip the bread in the cooking juices, shred the lamb, and you're all set.

Variations: You can use lamb shanks for this recipe instead of a leg of lamb, just wrap them individually. Or try substituting rosemary for the oregano and dill if you prefer.

Serves 4

4½lb leg of lamb
4 garlic cloves, sliced
¼ cup olive oil
juice of 2 lemons
1¼ cups finely chopped fresh dill
4 fresh oregano sprigs, or 1 teaspoon dried
2 teaspoons ground cinnamon
1 teaspoon ground cumin
sea salt
red wine vinegar (optional)

You will need some string or butcher's twine and some large pieces of parchment paper for this recipe.

Trim the lamb of excess fat and place on two large sheets of parchment paper. Using a small sharp knife, make incisions all over the leg and push in the garlic slices.

Mix the olive oil with the lemon juice and drizzle over the lamb. Mix together the herbs and spices and rub all over the meat, then season generously with sea salt.

Cover with another piece of parchment paper and fold the bottom pieces over the top piece to form a parcel, making sure everything is tucked in so you won't lose any cooking juices. Secure with string. Marinate in the fridge overnight or for at least 1 hour.

Remove the lamb from the fridge and let come up to room temperature while the oven heats to 350°F. Put the lamb in a roasting pan with the end of the leg slightly elevated to keep any juices from running out (I just rest it on the edge of the pan). Roast for 4 hours until meltingly tender.

Remove the lamb from the oven and rest for 30 minutes before unwrapping. Serve in the paper with all the delicious cooking juices (I like to add a splash of good-quality red wine vinegar to mine), shred the meat with forks, and allow guests to help themselves.

PULLED LAMB BURGERS

A little time-consuming to make, but once you've cooked the lamb it's all rock and roll! The recipe makes six but you might not want to share it all and make it for four instead. I like to serve the burgers with Fava Bean and Mint Hummus (page 132) and just a little watercress, but you could also serve them with Tzatziki (page 128) or Tahini Sauce (page 160). I make the Sesame Buns on page 156 to serve these in, but it's completely up to you how you serve them.

Serves 6

2 large Spanish onions
4½lb shoulder of lamb (on the bone)
½ cup olive oil, plus extra for drizzling (optional)
2 tablespoons dried oregano
2 tablespoons cumin seeds
2 tablespoons fennel seeds
a pinch of dried red pepper flakes
sea salt
4 garlic cloves, unpeeled
2½ cups cold water
½ cup finely chopped fresh mint leaves
¼ cup Cabernet Sauvignon vinegar

To serve:
bread, e.g. Sesame Buns, flatbread, focaccia,
 brioche, or challah rolls
sauce, e.g. Fava Bean and Mint Hummus

Preheat the oven to 325°F. Peel the onions and cut into ¼in slices. Place in a large roasting pan. Cut any excess fat off the lamb and place on top of the onions. Drizzle with olive oil then rub with the oregano, cumin and fennel seeds, and pepper flakes. Season generously with sea salt.

Add the garlic cloves and cold water to the pan and cover tightly with foil. Cook for 3¼ hours, then remove the foil and return to the oven. Cook for about 1 hour longer or until the lamb has colored and the meat is meltingly tender when prodded with a fork. Transfer the lamb to a wooden cutting board to rest for 20 minutes.

Meanwhile, place a sieve over a bowl and pour in the onions and cooking juices; skim the liquid of any fat. Roughly chop the onion slices and place in a large bowl. Squeeze the garlic cloves from their skins and add, along with the chopped mint. Using two forks, shred the lamb from the bone and place in the bowl with the onions, etc. Add the vinegar and enough reserved cooking juices to combine, mix well, and season with sea salt as needed.

Divide the mixture into six and form into patties. Place on one half of a baking sheet lined with parchment paper. Fold the paper over the patties, folding the edges over to loosely secure. If using immediately, increase the oven temperature to 350°F, place the burgers in the oven, and gently reheat for about 10–12 minutes while you prepare the bread by drizzling with olive oil and grilling slightly.

Carefully lift the patties off the paper and serve sandwiched between bread and topped with the sauce of your choice and some salad. Serve immediately.

If making ahead of time, you can wrap the patties individually in paper and warm in a hot oven the next day. I wrap them in paper so they don't dry out when reheating. For the ultimate cheeseburger, top the patties with a slice of feta then wrap in paper and reheat.

GRILLED LAMB CUTLETS WITH FENNEL TZATZIKI

Lamb cutlets cooked on a charcoal grill and eaten al fresco with a glass of retsina, personifies Greek cuisine. Teamed up with an herb and bean salad and Fennel Tzatziki, this is an easy barbecue dish to make and share.

Serves 4

3 garlic cloves, crushed
1 tablespoon dried oregano
½ cup olive oil
⅓ cup lemon juice
sea salt and freshly ground black pepper
12–16 lamb cutlets or rib chops (depending on your appetite!)
lemon wedges, to serve
White Bean Salad (page 136), to serve

Mix together the garlic, oregano, olive oil, and lemon juice in a non-reactive bowl, adding a generous pinch of salt and some pepper. Add the lamb cutlets and mix to combine evenly. Cover with plastic wrap and let marinate for at least 2 hours.

Preheat an outdoor grill or grill pan and cook the cutlets over high heat for 2–3 minutes on each side, depending on their thickness and your preferred "doneness." Transfer to a plate and serve with lemon wedges, fennel tzatziki, and White Bean Salad.

FENNEL TZATZIKI

1 teaspoon fennel seeds
1 garlic clove, crushed
sea salt
1½ cups Greek yogurt
½ fennel bulb
2 tablespoons lemon juice
a pinch of sugar

Toast the fennel seeds in a small pan until fragrant. Transfer to a mortar and pestle and grind along with the garlic and a generous pinch of sea salt. Transfer to a bowl and mix with the yogurt.

Trim the fennel of any tough outer layers and finely chop, along with any fronds. Mix with the yogurt, then add the lemon juice and sugar and taste for salt. Refrigerate for an hour or so before use to allow the flavors to infuse.

The tzatziki should keep well in the fridge for 3 days.

Variations: Add some chopped mint for a fresher flavor and/or a little finely grated orange zest—especially good with fish.

MOUSSAKA-STUFFED TOMATOES

Comforting moussaka is one of the loveliest things, but it often has a bad name originating from the tacky photographs outside touristy Greek restaurants, which often produce poor, greasy versions. Stuffed tomatoes always make me smile— a retro classic that outside of Greece you only find served at a relative's or in a deli, stuffed with some suspect couscous! Serve with a green salad or Lemon and Dill Braised Fava Beans (page 135). Again, as with most Greek food, the tomatoes will taste better the next day. Alternatively, you can prepare the tomatoes, make the filling and sauce ahead of time, and assemble on the day.

Serves 4–8 (makes 8 tomatoes)

1 eggplant
8 large beefsteak tomatoes
a pinch of superfine sugar
2 tablespoons olive oil, plus extra for drizzling
1 small onion, finely chopped
2 garlic cloves, finely chopped
14oz ground lamb
2 teaspoons ground cinnamon
a pinch of ground allspice
a pinch of dried oregano
¼ cup tomato paste
½ cup red or white wine
sea salt and freshly ground black pepper
¼ cup chopped fresh flat-leaf parsley
¾ cup chopped fresh mint

For the béchamel sauce:
1 tablespoon butter
2½ tablespoons flour
1¾ cups milk
a pinch of freshly grated nutmeg
¼ cup grated Kefalotyri or Parmesan

Preheat the oven to 400°F. Pierce the eggplant with a fork and roast on a baking sheet for about 30 minutes, until tender. Once cool enough to handle, peel and dice the flesh.

Meanwhile, slice the tops off the tomatoes and reserve. Scoop out most of the pulp with a teaspoon, being careful not to break the skin. Chop the pulp finely and drain, reserving the juices. Sprinkle the insides of the tomatoes with a little sugar and place cut-side down on a baking sheet until ready to use.

Heat the olive oil in a large frying pan over medium heat, add the onion and garlic, and cook until soft but without color. Turn up the heat, add the lamb, cinnamon, allspice, oregano, and tomato paste, and cook until the meat has browned. Add the eggplant, reserved tomato pulp and juice, and wine. Simmer for 5 minutes until the cooking juices are reduced. Season to taste, add the herbs, and set aside to cool.

To make the béchamel sauce, melt the butter in a small saucepan. Add the flour, stir, and cook over medium heat until the mixture turns a light sandy color. Whisk in the milk a little at a time and cook, whisking continuously, until the sauce thickens. Add the nutmeg and cheese and season to taste. Cover the surface with plastic wrap until ready to use to keep a skin from forming.

Reduce the oven temperature to 350°F. Fill the tomatoes with the lamb, being careful not to overfill them or they will split while cooking, and place in a snug-fitting baking dish. (If you don't have a small enough baking dish and the tomatoes are wobbling around, fill the gaps with some potato slices!) Spoon some béchamel over each one, top with a lid, and drizzle with a little olive oil. Pour a little water around them and bake, uncovered, for 30–35 minutes until the tomatoes are soft.

Remove from the oven and set aside to cool for 5 minutes before serving. To reheat the tomatoes if made in advance, place in a baking dish with a splash of water, cover, and warm through in a hot oven.

Variation: For a really quick alternative, omit the tomatoes, make the moussaka filling as above, and simply toss with some cooked Dried Fig Leaf Pasta Rags (page 116) or penne pasta, drizzle with béchamel, and serve.

STIFADO BRAISED BEEF BRISKET WITH BARLEY

A *stifado* is a traditional red wine stew that contains red wine vinegar and is made with small pearl onions. You could stifado anything really! Brisket is an economical cut of meat that needs to be slow braised. Serve with some wilted greens.

Variations: You could use beef cheeks, diced beef shank, or chuck steak instead of brisket.

Serves 4

¼ cup olive oil
2¼–3¼lb beef brisket, rolled
sea salt and freshly ground black pepper
4 onions, finely diced
4 garlic cloves, finely diced
2 tablespoons tomato paste
2 tablespoons sugar
2 bay leaves
1 large cinnamon stick
4 whole cloves
1 teaspoon black peppercorns
2 teaspoons coriander seeds
2 cups red wine
½ cup red wine vinegar
1 celery rib, finely chopped
1 small carrot, finely chopped
1 cup pearled barley
½ teaspoon ground cinnamon
3 tomatoes, peeled and finely chopped
¾ cup Kalamata black olives, pitted and chopped
½ cup chopped fresh mint
¾ cup chopped fresh flat-leaf parsley
½ cup Kefalotyri cheese or Pecorino, grated (optional)

Heat half the olive oil in a stockpot or saucepan large enough to hold the brisket snugly with enough liquid to cover. Season the beef with salt and pepper and sear over medium heat until colored on all sides, then set aside.

Add half the onions and half the garlic and cook until softened. Add the tomato paste and cook for another minute. Return the brisket to the pan along with the sugar, bay leaves, cinnamon, cloves, peppercorns, and coriander seeds. Pour in the wine and vinegar and enough water to cover the beef. Bring the liquid to a boil then reduce the heat to a simmer. Cover with parchment paper and weigh down the beef with a plate or lid. Cook for 2–3 hours, until the brisket is tender. Remove and set aside. Strain the cooking liquid into a clean pan or bowl and skim off any fat. (You can braise the brisket ahead of time; if doing so, pour the strained liquid over the beef, cool, and refrigerate.)

Heat the remaining oil in a large pan, add the remaining onions and garlic along with the celery and carrot, and sauté until softened. Add the barley and cinnamon and cook for 2 minutes. Pour in 3 cups of the cooking liquid and half of the tomatoes and bring to a boil, then reduce the heat to a simmer and cook until the barley is tender and most of the liquid has been absorbed. This should take 20–25 minutes, but cooking times may vary—it could take up to 40 minutes. Add a little more hot stock as necessary if the cooking times are longer.

While the barley is cooking, remove the twine from the brisket and cut into four to six slices. Place in a pan and cover with the remaining cooking liquid. Cover with tin foil and place over low heat to warm the beef through.

Add the remaining tomatoes and the olives to the barley, season with sea salt and black pepper, and stir in the herbs. Remove the beef from the pan and turn up the heat to reduce the remaining cooking liquid until thickened. Spoon over the beef and serve with the barley, sprinkled with cheese if using.

SLOW-BRAISED GOAT

Goats roam the Greek mountainsides, feeding on wild weeds, fresh herbs, and flowers, flavors that delicately enhance their milk and meat, which is as popular as lamb. Goat meat is sweet, succulent, delicately gamey, and meltingly tender.

A great source of protein, iron, and omega-3, and low in cholesterol, goat makes a great alternative to lamb as well as being ethical too. Billy goats that would otherwise be slaughtered (as their mothers' milk is more profitable sold) are now being reared for their meat, which is finally gaining slow popularity in the US.

I've slow-braised the meat here but it's also delicious spit-roasted, broiled, or dry-cured, another Greek speciality (see page 56). If time permits, make the dish the day before to allow the flavors to develop and then gently warm throughout the day.

Goat meat suppliers:

Try visiting your local butcher to purchase goat meat, or order online at elkusa.com, canyongoat. com, or localharvest.org

Serves 4–6

2 onions, coarsely chopped
2 carrots, coarsely chopped
2 celery ribs, coarsely chopped
a good glug of olive oil
3¼lb goat shoulder, on the bone
sea salt and freshly ground black pepper
2 garlic cloves, finely chopped
2 teaspoons fennel seeds, lightly crushed
1 teaspoon coriander seeds, lightly crushed
a pinch of dried red pepper flakes
2 teaspoons dried oregano
3 tablespoons tomato paste
1¼ cups red wine
2 quarts chicken stock
2 tablespoons red wine vinegar
1 cinnamon stick
1 bay leaf
5 thyme sprigs
2 rosemary sprigs
⅓ cup pitted Kalamata green olives, roughly chopped (optional)
2 tablespoons chopped fresh dill
2 tablespoons chopped fresh mint
3 tablespoons lemon juice
Feta Polenta, to serve (page 141)

Preheat the oven to 350°F.

Put the onions, carrots, and celery in a food processor and pulse until finely chopped. Alternatively, you could grate the vegetables. (These vegetables will form part of the sauce.)

Heat a little oil in a deep pan or Dutch oven large enough to hold the goat and stock. Season the goat with salt and pepper and sear over medium heat until well browned on each side. Set aside.

Add a dash more oil to the dish, turn up the heat, and add the chopped vegetables, garlic, fennel and coriander seeds, pepper flakes, and oregano. Cook until softened and without color. Stir in the tomato paste and cook for a minute longer while stirring. Add the wine and cook until reduced by half. Pour in the chicken stock and red wine vinegar, then add the cinnamon, bay leaf, thyme, and rosemary.

Return the seared goat to the pan or Dutch oven and bring almost to a boil. Cover the surface with parchment paper and top the pan with a lid, or cover it tightly with foil. Place in the oven and braise, turning the goat once, for 3½–4 hours or until the meat is very tender. Remove from the oven and let the goat cool in its braising liquid.

Discard the cinnamon stick, bay leaf, rosemary, and thyme from the liquid and lift out the goat. Skim the surface of fat and pour the liquid into a saucepan. Remove all the meat from the bone and pull or cut into small pieces, discarding the bone and any fatty bits. Return the meat to the sauce and heat gently over low heat.

Stir in the olives if using, along with the dill, mint, and lemon juice, and season with sea salt and pepper. Serve with the Feta Polenta. This would also be great with Dried Fig Leaf Pasta Rags (page 116) or Kalamata Olive Gnocchi (page 83).

DRIED FIG LEAF PASTA RAGS

The scent of fig leaves is heavenly, as is the flavor, which intensifies as the leaves dry. It amazes me that they're not traditionally used in Greek cuisine. You can, of course, dry fig leaves in the sun; otherwise, string them up in a bundle and hang them in the kitchen for a few days.

This pasta recipe uses egg yolks; I've included a couple of recipes in this book to take care of the leftover whites—Almond, Rose Water, and Chocolate Teacake Chimneys (page 194) and Apricot and Orange Blossom Meringues (page 196).

Variation: You can flavor the pasta dough with a little cinnamon, ground fennel seed, dried oregano, even lemon oil, but it's just as lovely "au naturel"! Just make sure that whatever spice you use is ground up enough so that the pasta dough rolls through the machine without sticking.

Serves 8–10 generously

½oz dried fig leaves
4 cups all-purpose flour or King Arthur bread flour, plus extra for dusting
9–10 free-range egg yolks (about 6oz)
2 whole free-range eggs
a dash of olive oil
fine semolina, for dusting

You will need a pasta machine for this recipe.

Tear the stems from the fig leaves and discard. Place the leaves in a food processor or spice grinder, process to a fine powder, and pass through a sieve.

If making the pasta by hand, combine the flour and powdered leaves in a bowl and mix well. Transfer to a clean work surface and make a well in the center. Add the yolks and whole eggs and whisk with a fork, keeping them within the flour walls. Starting from the outside, use the fork to mix in the egg while drizzling the olive oil into the flour a little at a time until a dough forms. Knead the dough for about 10 minutes until it feels smooth and elastic.

You can also make your dough in a food processor. Process the flour and powdered fig leaves together in the bowl until well combined. Then, with the motor running, add the yolks, whole eggs, and olive oil; blend until the mixture comes together and resembles bread crumbs. Transfer to the work surface and knead as above.

Wrap the dough in plastic wrap and rest in the fridge for an hour before using.

Lightly dust your work surface with flour. Cut the pasta dough in half (keep the remaining piece well wrapped up to prevent it from drying out) and roll it out to a rectangle about ¼in thick. With the pasta machine on its thickest setting, feed the dough through. Fold each edge into the center to form a rectangle and feed through the machine again, repeating three times. Then feed through once more without folding. Adjust the setting by one notch and repeat.

Continue in this way, changing the setting by one notch each time. The dough will get progressively smoother and more elastic. You may need to cut your dough in half if it's getting too long to handle. Repeat until you are one notch away from the thinnest setting, then cut the dough into rough pieces, or "rags," about 3in in surface area.

Place on a baking sheet lined with parchment paper and sprinkled with semolina (the semolina will stop the rags from sticking together). You can place another layer on top. Repeat with the remaining dough.

Rest the pasta for 30 minutes before cooking, or keep it in the fridge uncovered and use within two days. Alternatively, you can freeze it; let the pasta dry, then freeze it on baking sheets before transferring to a container—you can then use it directly from the freezer, making sure you allow a little extra time (up to a minute longer) when cooking.

To cook, bring a large saucepan of salted water to a boil, shake off any excess semolina, add the pasta rags to the pan, and cook for about 1½–2 minutes until al dente. (I always cook mine in a spaghetti basket so I can take them out the minute they're ready.) Unless your pot is huge, you may need to cook the rags in batches so as not to overcrowd the pan. I always save a little of the pasta water to add to my sauce. Toss with your prepared sauce and serve immediately—see page 118 for a recipe suggestion.

DRIED FIG LEAF PASTA RAGS WITH ROAST TOMATOES, SERRANO HAM, FIGS, AND CHEESE

At the height of summer, figs are at their best, as are tomatoes, so it seems natural to put them together. Figs alone seemed too obvious to add to the pasta, and I wanted to add another flavor and color. Here the ham and cheese give a salty element to what would have otherwise been quite a sweet pasta. I'm really proud of this dish—it was buzzing around in my head for a month until I got my hands on some fig leaves. The idea became a reality that didn't disappoint.

Serves 4

Lemon and Oregano Roasted Tomatoes (page 145)
a glug of extra-virgin olive oil
½ batch of Dried Fig Leaf Pasta Rags (page 116)
sea salt and freshly ground black pepper
6 slices of Serrano ham or Prosciutto, torn
2 figs, cut into eighths
⅓ cup skin-on almonds
1¼ cups grated Kefalotyri or Pecorino, to serve

Pull the roasted tomatoes from the vine, discard the vine, and lightly crush them by hand. Heat a good glug of olive oil in a large frying pan and gently warm the tomatoes and add some of their lemon zest, raisins, and any cooking juices from the pan.

Cook the dried pasta rags as described on page 117 and toss with the tomatoes, adding a little of the pasta cooking water. Season with salt and pepper and toss with the ham, figs, and almonds. Serve immediately, topped with grated cheese.

SHEFTALIA WITH OR WITHOUT A TWIST!

Sheftalia is a traditional Cypriot "sausage" or, technically speaking, an oval-shaped meatball. My Dad cooks sheftalia on a charcoal grill at his taverna in the Troodos mountains. The view is so beautiful, as is the scent of pine trees that hovers in the clean, fresh mountain air. This inspired me to embrace the ingredients surrounding us by infusing the sheftalia with this gorgeous scent. Of course my Dad (Mr. Traditional!) thought I was completely crazy to suggest such a thing: "Why on earth would you want to do that?!" I'll leave the judgement up to you. Here's the traditional recipe, but should you feel the urge, follow my suggestion and skewer a tender sprig of pine needle through each sheftalia before cooking for a delicately enriched sausage that'll transport you to the top of a mountain! You could always try using a sprig of rosemary, which doesn't sound half as romantic, but is equally delicious!

Sheftalia is often served solo with a wedge of lemon or stuffed into pita bread with salad for the most delicious kebab. I sometimes make my Dad a little more crazy, and serve my pine- or rosemary-infused sheftalia with Quince Skordalia (page 131)—after all, the boat's already rocked!

Serves 4 (makes 14)

7oz caul fat
2 medium onions or 1 large, grated or finely chopped
9oz ground pork
9oz ground lamb
½ bunch finely chopped fresh flat-leaf parsley
1 tablespoon finely chopped fresh mint or ½ teaspoon dried mint
¼ teaspoon ground cinnamon
¼ cup fresh bread crumbs or 2 slices of bread soaked in a little water then squeezed dry
sea salt and freshly ground black pepper
10 pine needle or rosemary sprigs, stripped of leaves (optional)

To serve:
lemon wedges
green salad
Quince Skordalia (optional), see comment on left

Wash the caul fat under running cold water until the water runs clear, then let soak while you prepare the sheftalia.

Mix the onions, meat, parsley, mint, cinnamon, and bread together and season with a generous pinch of salt and pepper. Knead well until combined. Cook a little of the meat to check the seasoning if you're unsure, then roll the mixture into 2in-long oval sausages.

Drain the caul fat and lay it flat on a work surface. Cut it into squares about 3 x 3in. Place the meat mixture at the edge of each square and fold the caul fat over the meat to encase. Fold in both sides, then roll up to enclose completely. If you want the "pine effect," now's the time to pierce each sheftalia horizontally with a sprig of pine needle (or rosemary).

Refrigerate for an hour to firm up before threading four to five sheftalia widthwise onto a double-pronged skewer or two metal skewers to create the same effect (this will keep them from spinning). Cook on a charcoal barbecue, or under a preheated medium-high broiler for about 15–20 minutes, turning frequently, until they are cooked through and browned.

Serve with lemon wedges, salad, and maybe some Quince Skordalia, if you like.

BAKED EGGS WITH GREEK SAUSAGE, TOMATOES, AND MINT

Inspired by the Tunisian dish Shakshuka. Serve with Sumac Flatbreads (page 159) for a hearty breakfast, brunch, or light lunch with a crisp green salad.

Loukaniko is a Greek lamb and pork sausage, flavored with fennel and orange zest. Soutzouki is a deliciously spicy and piquant beef and lamb sausage flavored with cumin, pepper, garlic, and sumac. Substitute with merguez sausages if you can't find them.

Variation: You can omit the sausage and replace with some charred eggplant. Pierce an eggplant all over with a fork and cook over a gas flame, turning regularly, until charred all over and tender. Alternatively, place under a hot broiler. Cool, halve, and scoop out the flesh with a spoon. Roughly chop the flesh and drain in a colander to get rid of the bitter juices. Add to the tomatoes and cook as directed.

Serves 4

4 tablespoons olive oil
2 loukaniko or 9oz soutzouki sausages, sliced
3 garlic cloves, finely chopped
a pinch of dried red pepper flakes
½ teaspoon ground cumin
1 tablespoon tomato paste
5 large ripe tomatoes, peeled and diced
  (or 2 x 14oz cans of tomatoes, crushed)
sea salt and freshly ground black pepper
8 free-range eggs (or 4 if you only want 1 each)
⅔ cup feta, crumbled (optional)
2 tablespoons roughly chopped fresh mint

Heat half the oil in a large frying pan. Add the sliced sausages and cook over medium heat until browned, then drain and set aside. Add the garlic to the pan and cook over low heat, adding a little more oil if necessary, until fragrant. Add the pepper flakes, cumin, and tomato paste and cook, stirring continuously, for a minute. Add the tomatoes and sausage slices and simmer over low heat for 10–15 minutes until thickened. Season with sea salt and black pepper.

Make eight (or four) "dents" in the sauce and break an egg into each. Turn the heat to low and sprinkle with feta (if using). Partly cover the pan and cook until the egg whites are set (about 5–7 minutes). Remove from the heat, sprinkle with mint, and serve in the pan.

BUBBLE AND SQUEAK

In Cockney rhyming slang, Greeks are known as "Bubble and Squeaks," so I couldn't let the opportunity to include this recipe slip! Bubble and squeak is a great way to use up any leftover vegetables from a roast dinner and is perfect for brunch with a poached egg perched on top. Add crispy fried bacon to the scallions if you want to make it a bit more substantial, or serve it with slices of ham, fennel salami, or cold turkey for a perfect family brunch.

Variations: Add some ground roasted coriander seeds to the mixture or some chopped mint. You could also try adding some finely sliced fennel to the scallions when cooking. Serve sprinkled with dried red pepper flakes or chile oil and a spoon of Greek yogurt.

Serves 4

1lb 2oz Russet potatoes, peeled and cut into even-sized chunks
a dash of milk
7 tablespoons unsalted butter
sea salt and freshly ground black pepper
1lb 2oz chard, spinach, or cavolo nero (or a mixture),
   stalks removed
¼ cup olive oil
4 scallions, finely chopped
2 garlic cloves, finely chopped
¾ cup pitted black olives, roughly chopped
1 teaspoon dried oregano
⅔ cup feta, crumbled
½ bunch finely chopped fresh flat-leaf parsley
a pinch of sumac

To serve:
1 lemon, cut into wedges
4 poached free-range eggs (optional)

Put the potatoes into a large saucepan of cold salted water, bring to a boil, and cook until tender. Drain, mash with a potato masher or pass through a ricer, then beat in the milk and half the butter and mix until smooth. Season with sea salt and black pepper.

Meanwhile, blanch the leaves in a pan of boiling water for 2 minutes, refresh in ice-cold water, and drain. Squeeze out excess water—wringing them out in an old, clean kitchen towel is the best way to do this!

Heat the olive oil in a large, nonstick frying pan, add the scallions and garlic, and cook until softened. Add the greens, olives, and oregano and cook for 5 minutes, stirring occasionally. Mix in the mashed potato (and any chopped-up leftover vegetables if you have them) and arrange in an even layer. If you prefer, shape into individual cakes.

Cook for around 10 minutes over medium heat until a lovely golden crust forms on the bottom. Carefully flip the potatoes over (the easiest way to do this is to slide them onto a plate, place the frying pan over the uncooked side, and flip the plate over). Add the remaining butter to the pan, melt, and cook for another 5 minutes. Sprinkle with feta cheese, parsley, and sumac; serve immediately topped with lemon wedges and poached eggs, if using.

SLOW-BRAISED PORK BELLY WITH WILTED GREENS, OLIVES, AND CAPERS

This is a one-pot wonder. Delicious served with crusty bread, or else make it more substantial by adding a can of butter beans or black-eyed peas or serving it with Feta Polenta (page 141).

Variation: If you prefer, you can cook the pork (covered) in the oven instead of simmering on the stove. Cook for the same length of time at 350°F.

Serves 4

3¼lb piece of pork belly
sea salt and freshly ground black pepper
a good glug of olive oil
1 onion, finely chopped
1 leek, finely chopped
1 small fennel bulb, finely sliced
4 garlic cloves, finely chopped
6 salted anchovies, finely chopped
1½ cups white wine
3½ cups chicken stock
18oz–1¼lb mixed leafy greens, such as a mix of spinach, chard (red or green), kale, dandelion, or similar, torn into rough pieces
2¼ cups broccoli, roughly chopped
⅓ cup capers, rinsed
¾ cup pitted green olives, roughly chopped
juice of ½ lemon, to taste
¾ cup finely chopped fresh flat-leaf parsley

Remove the skin from the pork belly and cut the meat into four equal pieces; season each with salt. Heat a little olive oil in a large, heavy-bottomed saucepan. Add the pork and cook over high heat until browned on each side. Transfer to a plate.

Add the onion, leek, fennel, garlic, and anchovies to the pan and cook over medium heat for about 10 minutes, or until the onion and leeks are tender. Return the pork to the pan, add the wine, and heat until reduced by half.

Add the chicken stock (this should be about ¾in short of covering the pork) then bring to a boil, cover, and simmer for 1½ hours.

Add the greens, broccoli, capers, and olives and stir to combine the leaves with the cooking liquid. Cover and simmer for another 30 minutes, by which time the pork should be tender and the greens and broccoli wilted. If necessary, continue to cook the pork, covered, until the meat is tender (the time taken will depend on the thickness of the belly); if you want to serve the pork with butter beans or black-eyed peas, add them now. Remove the pork and let rest in a warm place.

Add the lemon juice and season the greens to taste. Stir in the parsley and serve in deep bowls.

³/ SALADS & SIDE PLATES

TZATZIKI

Eat this by itself with toasted pita or flatbread or just about anything else in this book! I love it in a sandwich with slow-roasted lamb or smoked peppered mackerel.

Variations: You could use mint instead of dill or replace the cucumber with ¼ cup of grated cooked beets. Radishes also work well. Alternatively, add some chopped watercress and sorrel to the cucumber mix. For Fennel Tzatziki, see page 108.

Makes about 1¼ cups

½ cucumber
sea salt
1–2 garlic cloves
1 tablespoon extra-virgin olive oil
2 teaspoons red wine vinegar
1 tablespoon finely chopped fresh dill
⅔ cup Greek yogurt

Peel the cucumber, cut it in half lengthwise, and scoop out the seeds with a teaspoon. Finely chop or grate then place in a colander, sprinkle with a pinch of sea salt, and let drain for 10 minutes.

While the cucumber drains, crush the garlic with a pinch of sea salt until puréed. Put in a bowl and mix with the olive oil, vinegar, dill, and yogurt.

Using your hands, squeeze any excess water from the cucumber and add to the yogurt. Stir well and refrigerate for 1–2 hours to allow the flavors to infuse.

TZATZIKI LABNE

Strain 2½ cups Greek yogurt in a sieve lined with clean cheesecloth or muslin. Bring the sides together, place a plate on top, and weigh down with a can. Place over a bowl and let strain for 3 hours or overnight. Place the strained yogurt in a bowl and continue with the recipe above. Roll the tzatziki into small balls, drizzle with olive oil, and roll in chopped herbs such as parsley, dill, mint, or a combination of these or some roasted pulsed pine nuts and lemon zest.

TARAMASALATA

If you've only ever tried taramasalata that's bright pink in color and from a supermarket, tasting this recipe will be a complete revelation. Ask your fishmonger to order you some smoked cod's roe if they don't have any in stock.
I love taramasalata with pan-fried scallops and fennel salad, but my guilty pleasure is taramasalata and french fries! If you have any left over, use it to make Salt Cod Croquettes (page 45).

Makes about 1¼ cups

7oz smoked cod's roe
1-2 slices white bread, about 1½oz, crusts removed
¼ cup warm water, plus extra for soaking
¾ cup olive oil (extra-virgin will make it bitter)
2–3 tablespoons freshly squeezed lemon juice

Cut the roe in half lengthwise and scoop out the flesh with a spoon into a food processor or blender.

Put the bread in a bowl and soak in a little warm water to soften for about 5 minutes. Squeeze out the excess water and place the bread in the processor with the roe. Pulse to mix. With the motor running, gradually add the olive oil. Add 2 tablespoons of the lemon juice and pulse to mix. Add the water and pulse again.

Taste the taramasalata and add a little more lemon juice if you prefer. Transfer to a container and refrigerate for 30 minutes before serving.

SKORDALIA

Served as a dip or an accompaniment to white meat, fish, seafood (particularly fried calamari), and vegetables such as zucchini, artichokes, and beets, skordalia can be made with potato or bread with the addition, depending on regional differences, of walnuts, almonds, and sometimes chestnuts or pistachios. Basically, every region will tell you, I mean argue, that theirs is the best! Potatoes give it a smoother consistency, while the bread version is a bit grainier. I also like to experiment with other flavors, such as parsnip, white beans, fava beans, cauliflower, beets, even quince. For a richer skordalia, beat in a whole egg once the skordalia is made.

BREAD SKORDALIA

3 slices of white bread crusts removed
3 garlic cloves
1 teaspoon sea salt
1–2 tablespoons red wine vinegar
¼ cup olive oil
sea salt and freshly ground black pepper

Soak the bread in cold water until saturated, then squeeze out excess water. Crush the garlic with the salt in a pestle and mortar until puréed. Put the garlic, bread, and vinegar in a food processor. Blend until smooth, then slowly add the oil with the motor still running. Season with salt and pepper, cover, and refrigerate until required.

The garlic will intensify in flavor the longer you leave it. Use within a day or two.

POTATO SKORDALIA

I've included three different skordalia-making methods for you to choose from: by hand, food processor, or pestle and mortar. To achieve the best results, follow the age-old practice of making the potato skordalia with a pestle and mortar. The consistency will be so much better than if done using a food processor, which tends to make the potatoes a little "gloopy."

9oz potatoes, peeled and cut into cubes
sea salt and freshly ground black pepper
3–4 garlic cloves
½ teaspoon sea salt
1 tablespoon red wine vinegar, or lemon juice if you prefer
¾ cup extra-virgin olive oil (or a blend of extra-virgin and olive oil)

Cook the potatoes in salted water until tender, about 15 minutes; drain and mash until smooth. Pound the garlic with the sea salt in a pestle and mortar until puréed, then pick a method from the three below.

By hand method:
Add the garlic paste and vinegar to the mashed potatoes and gradually beat in the olive oil, mixing vigorously with a wooden spoon. Season with salt and pepper and serve at room temperature.

Pestle and mortar method:
Add a little cooked potato to the crushed garlic in the pestle and mortar and pound until smooth. Add the vinegar and a little oil and repeat, adding a little more potato and oil, until they are both incorporated. Season with salt and pepper and serve at room temperature.

Food processor method:
Place the pounded garlic and salt in a food processor with the drained, cooked, warm potatoes along with the vinegar and half the oil. Blend until smooth. With the motor still running, gradually add the remaining oil. Season with salt and pepper and serve at room temperature.

PARSNIP SKORDALIA

Puréed parsnips have a velvety smooth texture and lend themselves well to bold garlicky and lemon flavors. This is delicious with Rabbit Baklava (page 93) and Roast Spatchcock Chicken (page 86).

2¼lb parsnips, trimmed, peeled, and cored
3 garlic cloves, peeled
2 cups milk
juice of 1 lemon, or to taste
½ cup blanched almonds (optional)
½ cup olive oil
sea salt

Cut the parsnips into ¼in even-sized pieces and put them in a saucepan. Add 1 garlic clove and cover with milk. Cook until the parsnips are tender (about 15–20 minutes), drain, reserving 3 tablespoons of the cooking liquid, and put in a blender. Add the remaining garlic, half the lemon juice, reserved cooking liquid, and blend until almost smooth. Add the almonds (if using) and, with the motor running slowly, drizzle in the oil until incorporated. Season with sea salt and adjust the lemon juice to taste. Let cool and serve at room temperature.

POMEGRANATE SKORDALIA

I've chosen to enrich this skordalia with a splash of pomegranate molasses. If you want a lighter option, just mix the pomegranate molasses with some yogurt and garlic.

4 slices of white bread, crusts removed
4 garlic cloves, finely chopped
1 teaspoon sea salt
1 tablespoon pomegranate molasses
¼–⅓ cup olive oil (not extra-virgin)
sea salt and freshly ground black pepper

Soak the bread in cold water until saturated, then squeeze out excess water. Crush the garlic with the salt in a pestle and mortar until smooth. Place the garlic salt and bread in a food processor. Blend until smooth and add the pomegranate molasses, then slowly add the oil with the motor still running. Season with salt and pepper, cover, and refrigerate until required.

BREAD SKORDALIA WITH NUTS

Replace 1 slice of the bread in the Bread Skordalia recipe with some crushed walnuts or pine nuts, and follow the recipe as instructed, adding a drop more vinegar to taste to cut the richness of the nuts. Some people prefer to use a white wine vinegar or lemon juice; it's entirely up to personal taste.

QUINCE SKORDALIA

Add a couple of tablespoons of quince paste to either the Potato or Bread Skordalia recipe.

FAVA BEAN AND MINT HUMMUS

This is great as a dip but even better slathered between grilled bread and topped with a Pulled Lamb Burger! (You'll find the recipe for the burger on page 106.)

Variations: Replace the fava beans with cooked asparagus or fresh peas.

Serves 4–6

1lb 2oz fresh fava beans (shelled weight), or frozen if
   not in season
sea salt
½ cup olive oil
¼ cup finely chopped fresh mint
¼ cup finely chopped fresh dill
juice of 1 lemon

Cook the fresh beans in lightly salted boiling water until tender (about 5 minutes, but do check as the time will vary depending on the size and age of the beans), then drain and plunge into ice-cold water. Slide the beans out of their skins, transfer to a food processor, and pulse to form a rough purée. If using frozen fava beans, put them in cold water to defrost, then slide them from their skins—no cooking is required and the color is a lot more vibrant.

With the motor still running, gradually pour in the olive oil, then add the herbs, half the lemon juice, and a large pinch of salt. Pulse-blend (I like to leave mine a little chunky) then taste. You might want to add a little more lemon juice or salt. Mix and transfer to a container. Refrigerate until required.

LEMON AND DILL BRAISED FAVA BEANS

I like to visit Eleni (pictured opposite) whenever I go to the village. I've never had a conversation with her—she speaks no English and my Greek's terrible. I know she'd have a thousand stories to tell. Her vision is greatly impaired but it doesn't keep her from her chores. On the day I went to visit, she was prepping the beans grown in her garden. There's something very therapeutic about shelling fava beans.

These are divine with Grilled Lamb Cutlets (page 108) or Pickled Chicken (page 54) and Tzatziki (page 128). They are best made the day before, and it's well worth the effort to shell the beans. Serve at room temperature, sprinkled with a little feta.

Serves 4–8 generously

4½lb fresh fava beans in their pods, or 2¼lb frozen
5 tablespoons extra-virgin olive oil
1 onion, finely chopped
1 garlic clove, finely chopped
a pinch of sugar
a pinch of sea salt
1¼ cups chicken stock or water
juice of 1 lemon
a small bunch of finely chopped fresh dill
sea salt and freshly ground black pepper

Shell the beans and remove their outer coats. If using fresh beans, the easiest way to do this is to blanch them for a minute in boiling water then refresh in cold water. If using frozen, simply defrost in cold water then slide the beans out of their shells.

Heat the oil in a large saucepan and gently cook the onion until softened without color. Add the garlic, sugar, and salt and cook for another 2 minutes. Add the beans and stock or water and simmer over low heat for about 20 minutes, until the beans are tender and most of the liquid has been absorbed. Remove from the heat.

Stir in the lemon juice and dill, season to taste with salt and pepper, and let stand for an hour before serving—better still, leave overnight in the fridge.

LEMON AND DILL BRAISED ARTICHOKES AND FAVA BEANS

If you would like to add some artichokes to your beans, you will need to prepare two globe artichokes ahead of time. Place the artichokes in a large pot of acidulated water (water with a dash of vinegar or lemon juice) with a pinch of salt. Cover with paper and weigh down with a plate or small lid. Cook for about 20 minutes until tender and the tough outer leaves can be easily removed; the timing will depend on the size of your artichokes. Remove all the tough outer leaves and trim the stalks, cut in half, remove the fuzzy chokes with a spoon, and cut each half into thirds. Add the artichokes when cooking the onion; continue with the recipe as above, adding a little extra stock if required.

WHITE BEAN SALAD

Serve alongside Grilled Lamb Cutlets and Fennel Tzatziki (page 108). The combination is so fresh and light. The smaller the white bean the better for this recipe—Arrocina, tiny Spanish white beans, are ideal, but cannellini, fresh or dried, make a suitable alternative.

Serves 4–6

1½ cups fresh flat-leaf parsley
¾ cup fresh mint leaves
½ cup cooked white beans or ⅓ cup dried beans soaked overnight and cooked until tender
2 scallions, finely sliced
½ fennel bulb (if making the Tzatziki, use the remaining half), finely chopped
1 vine-ripened tomato, finely diced (no need to peel or deseed it)
1 teaspoon ground cinnamon
½ teaspoon ground allspice
sea salt
juice of ½ lemon
¼ cup olive oil
1 teaspoon sumac (optional)

Using a very sharp knife, slice the parsley leaves and stems as thinly as possible, working your way down from leaf to stem end. Repeat with the mint and put both herbs in a bowl. Combine with the beans, scallions, fennel, tomato, cinnamon, and allspice; season with sea salt and dress with lemon juice and olive oil. Refrigerate to allow the flavors to infuse before serving at room temperature, sprinkled with sumac.

Variations: Substitute some or all of the beans with lentils, quinoa, or blanched fava beans or peas. Or add finely chopped cucumber, olives, or capers.

WHITE BEAN, ARTICHOKE, AND BASIL HUMMUS

We used to make a "hummus of the day" at the restaurant and serve it in a little flower pot with crudités. The moment we sent one out, everyone would order it because they looked so pretty. Serve with hot pita or crusty bread.

Serves 4–6

6oz grilled artichoke hearts marinated in olive oil (from a 7oz jar)
½ cup cooked butter beans
2 garlic cloves, finely chopped
2 tablespoons lemon juice
2 tablespoons fresh basil or Greek basil leaves, roughly chopped (reserve a few small leaves for garnish)
1 teaspoon sea salt
3 tablespoons artichoke oil (from the jar)
a little extra-virgin olive oil for drizzling (or see note below)
freshly ground black pepper
crudités or bread of your choice, to serve

Drain the artichokes, reserving the oil, and roughly chop. Put them in a food processor along with the butter beans and garlic and pulse-blend. Add the lemon juice, basil, salt, and oil and blend until smooth. Spoon into a shallow bowl. Using the back of a spoon, make a shallow indent in the hummus. Top with a little olive oil and black pepper and sprinkle with (Greek) basil leaves. Serve with crudités or bread.

Variations: Drizzle the finished hummus with a little truffle oil, or top with wafer-thin slices of fresh truffle—taking your hummus to decadent heights!

FAVA PURÉE

One of the most famous recipes of Santorini, this is made from yellow split peas, which have their very own PDO (Protected Designation of Origin). It is velvety smooth in texture with a rich earthy flavor that's heightened with olive oil and lemon juice. The quality of dried peas can differ dramatically so always try to look for the best. I love to serve this with slow-roasted rabbit, caper leaves, and an Ouzo Lemon Dressing (page 161). Alternatively, serve as a dip/accompaniment to roast meats/grilled fish, or pita bread.

Serves 4–8

1lb yellow split peas
2 shallots, peeled and halved
3 garlic cloves, peeled
1 bay leaf
5 thyme sprigs
½ cup extra-virgin olive oil, plus extra for drizzling
juice of ½ lemon, or to taste
sea salt and freshly ground black pepper

To serve:
red onion/scallions/capers
lemon wedges

Put the split peas in a fine colander and wash under cold running water, picking out any stones. Put the split peas, shallots, garlic, bay, and thyme in a large saucepan, cover with water, and bring to a boil, skimming off the foam that floats on the top. Reduce the heat to a simmer and cook until the peas are soft and almost all the water has been absorbed; this can take about 1–1½ hours. (Skim off the foam regularly and stir occasionally, adding a little more water if necessary.)

Drain the peas and reserve a little of the cooking liquid. Discard the shallots, bay, and thyme sprigs, but keep the garlic. Put the peas in a blender with the garlic and, with the motor still running, slowly pour in the olive oil followed by the lemon juice. Season with sea salt and black pepper. If the mixture is a little thick, add some of the reserved cooking liquid. It should have the consistency of soft hummus, but it will thicken up once cooled. Refrigerate until required (it will keep for 3–4 days).

Serve the Fava Purée lukewarm, drizzled with olive oil, a hunk of sesame bread, and any of the following sprinkled on the top: finely chopped red onions, sliced scallions, caper leaves, capers, or crispy capers. Serve with lemon wedges.

Variations: Sometimes I like to add a dash of Cabernet Sauvignon vinegar to the purée and some extra raw, crushed garlic. You can easily adapt this recipe to your taste.

CYPRUS FRIES

In my opinion, Cyprus potatoes make the best fries in the world! Their distinctive red skin and unique taste comes from the mineral-rich, red soil in which the potatoes are grown. Unfortunately, they are only harvested twice a year, which makes me appreciate them all the more. Greeks love these potatoes roasted with oregano, olive oil, and lemon juice, which results in soft, aromatic and sticky potatoes brimming with flavor. If you're lucky enough to come across Cyprus potatoes, I don't think you'll be disappointed with the results. Serve with Taramasalata (page 129) for a heavenly treat!

Serves as many people that you feel you want to share with—perhaps 4

2¼lb Cyprus potatoes or Russet or Yukon Gold, if you can't get ahold of them, peeled
vegetable or sunflower oil, or even a light olive oil
sea salt, or a flavored salt such as my Oregano Lemon Salt (page 161)

Cut the potatoes into even-sized batons and put in a large bowl of cold water. Rinse under running water until the water runs clear. Drain and dry thoroughly in a cloth.

Heat the oil in a deep-fat fryer or large heavy-bottomed saucepan to 300°F and blanch the potatoes in batches for about 12 minutes (the time will depend on your preferred fry size); they need to be tender but not browned. It's really important that you blanch each batch for exactly the same amount of time so that they cook evenly when refrying. Drain well and set aside to cool. You can now refrigerate the fries for up to two days before serving.

When ready to serve, heat the oil to 350°F and refry in batches until crisp and golden. Drain on paper towels and sprinkle with salt. Always remember, never leave your fry pan or fryer unguarded.

KALAMATA POTATO MASH

I love the combination of creamy and salty and this indulgent mash is a great side to many of the dishes in this book.

Serves 4

2¼lb potatoes, such as red-skinned, Russet, or Yukon Gold, peeled and cut into even-sized chunks
⅔ cup heavy cream
9 tablespoons unsalted butter
12 black Kalamata olives, pitted and chopped
sea salt and freshly ground black pepper
extra-virgin olive oil, for drizzling

Bring the potatoes to a boil in a saucepan of salted water and cook for 25–30 minutes or until tender (or you could steam them). Drain in a colander, then pass through a potato ricer or sieve, or mash thoroughly by hand.

Heat the cream and butter until almost boiling, then gradually beat the liquid into the potatoes until you have a smooth purée. Add the olives and mix well. Taste before seasoning with salt (remember the olives are salty) and pepper. Drizzle with olive oil and serve.

Variations: You could flavor the cream with fresh oregano sprigs. Or try using green olives and finish with a little crumbled feta.

STIFADO FONDANT POTATOES

I have fond memories of many hours spent as an apprentice turning potatoes into eight-sided barrels for fondant potatoes! Nowadays, it's the trend to cut them into cylinders instead, as I've done here, although you could of course cut them into rectangular blocks. As they cook they'll soak up all the stock and glisten in the butter. Breaking with tradition, I've added a stifado twist—"stifado" means a stew flavored with red wine and aromatics, in which beef or rabbit are usually braised. The flavor is divine, and I thought it would be great applied to potatoes.

Serves 4–8

½ cup red wine
¾ cup chicken stock
1 cinnamon stick
1 bay leaf
2 large red-skinned potatoes, peeled
2 garlic cloves, chopped
2 thyme sprigs, picked
3 tablespoons unsalted butter
a dash of red wine vinegar
a handful of chopped fresh flat-leaf parsley
8 black Kalamata olives, pitted and roughly chopped

Preheat the oven to 375°F. Pour the red wine and chicken stock into a saucepan, add the cinnamon and bay leaf, and bring to a boil.

Meanwhile, use a pastry cutter to cut the potatoes into 1½in round, 1¼in deep cylinders. Trim the edges straight and stand them in a shallow ovenproof frying pan or baking dish in which they will fit snugly. Pour in enough stock to half cover the potatoes. Add the cinnamon and bay from the pan, along with the garlic and thyme. Dot with butter and cook, basting once, for about 50 minutes, or until the potatoes are tender and have absorbed most of the stock. (The cooking time will depend on the thickness of your potatoes, so it's best to check after 30 minutes.)

Remove from the oven and toss the potatoes with the red wine vinegar, parsley, and olives. Serve warm.

Variation: Toss the potatoes with some chopped cherry tomatoes and crumbled feta.

FETA POLENTA

Soft polenta makes a great alternative to potatoes or pasta; it's quick and easy to make, too. I like to jazz it up with the addition of some feta cheese. Serve it as an accompaniment to Slow-braised Goat (page 114), Slow-braised Pork Belly (page 125), or Calamari, Eggplant, and Tomato Braise (page 39).

Serves 4

2 cups milk
1 bay leaf
2 garlic cloves, bruised
1¼ cups water
5½oz instant polenta
1 tablespoon butter
⅓ cup feta, crumbled
sea salt and freshly ground black pepper
extra-virgin olive oil, to drizzle

Heat the milk, bay leaf, garlic, and water in a saucepan until almost boiling. Turn off the heat and let infuse for about 20 minutes.

Skim off any skin from the milk and fish out the bay leaf and garlic. Reheat until simmering, then add the polenta in a thin, steady stream, whisking continuously. Whisk until thick (2–3 minutes) then remove from the heat and stir in the butter and feta. Season generously with salt and pepper and serve immediately, drizzled with olive oil.

Variations: Try experimenting with the flavors by adding a little chopped thyme, rosemary, or sage, or a pinch of ground cinnamon or dried red pepper flakes. Or replace the feta with some grated Kefalotyri, Pecorino, or Parmesan, or even a little blue cheese. If you've made the Goat's Milk Ricotta (page 32), you can use the residue milk for cooking the polenta (topping off with water to make 2 cups). If you prefer a lighter version, replace the milk with stock or water.

PEACHY GREEK PANZANELLA

Panzanella is a bread salad that's bursting with flavor—in my first book, The Modern Vegetarian, *I included a watermelon version. It's a great accompaniment to barbecued meat and fish or with a plate of Serrano ham or any other charcuterie and, of course, cheese—feta, chile-baked feta, or goat cheese.*

Variations: You can add many ingredients to this recipe. The saltiness of crumbled feta, for example, works really well with the sweet juicy peaches, as do charred green bell peppers. You could add some peppery arugula leaves or watercress, or olives and purslane. One more thing—you could even use sesame rusks instead of the bread. I guess I had best stop with the alternatives here or there'll be no room on the page for the recipe!

Serves 4–6

2 shallots
sea salt and freshly ground black pepper
¼ cup Cabernet Sauvignon vinegar
2 ripe peaches
olive oil, for drizzling
10 slices of Greek sesame bread, or ciabatta
2 garlic cloves, peeled
1lb 2oz cherry vine tomatoes, halved
a small bunch of fresh basil, leaves torn

For the dressing:
2 teaspoons dried oregano or thyme leaves
a pinch of sugar
¼ cup Cabernet Sauvignon/red wine vinegar
⅔ cup extra-virgin olive oil

Peel and halve the shallots lengthwise and thinly slice. Put in a small bowl, add a pinch of sea salt, and toss with the vinegar. Let marinate while you prepare the rest of the salad.

Preheat a grill pan while you cut the peaches into halves, then quarters. Drizzle the peaches with a little oil and place on the hot pan until charred on each side—do this over high heat as you want the peaches to take on a charred taste but still remain firm and juicy. Place on a plate in a single layer (if you pile them up they'll steam and continue to cook) and let cool.

Rub the bread with the garlic (do not discard the garlic), drizzle with olive oil, and place, in batches, on the hot pan until charred on each side. Set aside to cool.

Cut each peach quarter in half and put in a large bowl along with the tomatoes and basil. Tear the bread into pieces roughly the same size as the peaches and add to the bowl, along with the marinated shallots and their juices.

Finely chop the garlic and place in a separate bowl. Add the dressing ingredients and whisk to combine. Pour over the salad and toss to coat. Season with salt and pepper; allow the flavors to marinate for about 10 minutes before serving.

LEMON AND OREGANO ROASTED TOMATOES WITH KEFALOTYRI

Each summer my roommate grows hanging baskets of cherry vine tomatoes in our garden. There's always an abundance, so this is a great way of using them up. Full of flavor, they're great served on their own with crusty Greek bread or tossed into Dried Fig Leaf Pasta Rags with Serrano Ham, Figs, and Cheese (page 118).

Serves 4–6

1lb 2oz small vine-ripened tomatoes (walnut-sized)
2 teaspoons fennel seeds
½ cup raisins
4 strips of lemon zest, pith removed
6 oregano sprigs
a good glug of olive oil, plus extra to serve
sea salt and freshly ground black pepper
1 cup shaved Kefalotyri or Pecorino (optional)

Preheat the oven to 400°F. Place the tomatoes (still on the vine) in a single layer in a small roasting pan. Scatter with fennel seeds, raisins, lemon zest, and oregano and drizzle with olive oil. Roast the tomatoes until they're just about to burst, about 20–35 minutes.

Remove from the oven, place on a serving platter, and drizzle with olive oil and cooking juices. Sprinkle with salt and pepper and top with the cheese. Serve as a small plate or a side to accompany practically any dish in this book—they're so versatile—or serve with the Fig Leaf Pasta as suggested.

Variations: Add some sliced chile and replace the lemon zest with a little orange. Substitute the oregano with some rosemary or bay leaves, or try replacing the fennel with coriander seeds. If Kefalotyri or Pecorino are unavailable, crumble over a little feta.

HORTA SALAD

This wild greens salad is a classic dish made with a variety of foraged greens (horta) that are wilted and dressed with lemon and olive oil. It's a great accompaniment to any meal or can be served on its own topped with a little crumbled feta as a small plate.

Serves 4

1¾lb wild greens, such as a combination of spinach, chard, dandelion, beet leaves, curly endive, arugula, mustard, and amaranth
¼ cup lemon juice
6 tablespoons extra-virgin olive oil
sea salt and freshly ground black pepper

Clean and trim the greens, discarding the stems. Blanch the leaves in salted water for 3–5 minutes until wilted. (If using beet and chard leaves, you might want to give these a minute first before adding the other leaves.)

Whisk the lemon juice and oil together until amalgamated. Drain the leaves and add the dressing plus a little salt and pepper to taste. Toss and serve cold or at room temperature.

Some health-conscious Greeks are known to drink a glass of the greens' cooking liquid!

CELERIAC PURÉE

It's not the prettiest of vegetables, but what celeriac lacks in looks, it makes up for in flavor. Velvety smooth and comforting, this purée is the perfect accompaniment to Pickled Squab and Cherry Relish (page 52) or Slow-roasted Paper-wrapped Lamb (page 105). Celeriac is also fabulous roasted as you would a potato with olive oil, finished with a squeeze of lemon, capers, and some chopped dill or parsley.

Serves 4

1 medium celeriac, peeled and cut into small, even pieces
sea salt and freshly ground black pepper
⅔ cup heavy cream
¼ cup milk
2 tablespoons unsalted butter, diced

Put the celeriac in a saucepan, add a pinch of salt, and cover with cold water. Bring to a boil then reduce the heat to a simmer, cooking the celeriac until it's tender, about 10–15 minutes depending on the size of the pieces. Drain well and return to the heat for a minute or so to dry; pass through a sieve or ricer or mash while still warm.

Heat the cream and milk and beat into the warm celeriac, adding enough to make a consistency as smooth as mashed potatoes. Stir in the butter and season with salt and pepper. Alternatively, process the warm celeriac in a blender with the hot cream and milk and diced butter. Serve warm.

CINNAMON AND WALNUT POURGOURI

Pourgouri is the Cypriot name for bulgur or cracked wheat. A few pomegranate seeds or raisins (pre-soaked) would work well mixed into this, as would some chopped pickled red cabbage. It's a perfect accompaniment to Roast Partridge (page 96).

Serves 4–6

¼ cup olive oil or 2 tablespoons unsalted butter and 2 tablespoons olive oil
2 onions, halved and finely sliced
2 teaspoons ground cinnamon
1 cup pourgouri or bulgur
1¾ cups chicken stock or water
1 bay leaf
½ cup chopped walnuts
sea salt and freshly ground black pepper
2 tablespoons chopped fresh flat-leaf parsley
2 tablespoons chopped fresh mint (optional)

Heat the oil and butter, if using, in a large saucepan. Add the onions and cook over medium heat until caramelized; this will take about 15 minutes. Add the cinnamon and pourgouri and cook for 2 minutes, stirring to coat.

Add the stock or water, bay leaf, and half the walnuts to the pan and season with salt and pepper. Cover with a lid, reduce the heat to its lowest setting, and cook for 5 minutes. Turn off the heat and let the pourgouri cook in the residual heat for another 5 minutes.

Remove the lid, fluff with a fork, then add the remaining walnuts and herbs. Season to taste and serve warm.

TOMATO BULGUR PILAF

I was permanently broke as an apprentice and this recipe was something I loved because it was cheap to make, quick, and flavorful. I've added the fresh herbs—they were a luxury I couldn't afford in those days—and these days I serve the pilaf with grilled sardines or lamb, rather than with fish sticks, as I used to!

Serves 4

2 tablespoons olive oil or 2 tablespoons
   unsalted butter
1 onion, finely chopped
2 tablespoons tomato paste
a pinch of ground cinnamon
¾ cup bulgur wheat
¾ cup chicken stock or water
sea salt and freshly ground black pepper
2 tablespoons chopped fresh flat-leaf parsley
2 tablespoons chopped fresh mint

Heat the oil or butter in a large saucepan, add the onion, and cook over medium heat until the onion has colored. Add the tomato paste and cook for 1 minute, stirring continuously. Add the cinnamon and bulgur wheat and cook for a minute longer.

Add the stock or water and season with salt and pepper. Cover with plastic wrap or a lid, reduce the heat to its lowest setting, and cook for 10 minutes. Then turn off the heat and leave the bulgur to cook in the residual heat for another 5 minutes.

Remove the lid or plastic wrap, add the chopped herbs, season to taste, and serve warm.

LEMON PARSLEY SALAD

This is a simple salad to tantalize your taste buds. It's inspired by a cooking show I once watched on television in Tuscany. It goes beautifully with Sardine Keftedes (page 51), Paper-wrapped Leg of Lamb (page 105), or Whole Baked Snapper (page 74).

Serves 4

2 lemons
2 tablespoons capers, rinsed and roughly chopped
2 shallots, finely chopped
a pinch of sugar
a pinch of dried red pepper flakes
sea salt
1¼ cups fresh flat-leaf parsley (leaves only)
¼ cup extra-virgin olive oil

Cut the ends off the lemons, then peel and remove the membranes. Segment into a bowl, squeezing the membranes of any excess juice. Add the capers, shallots, superfine sugar, and pepper flakes, along with a generous pinch of sea salt. Mix to combine. Toss with the parsley and olive oil, taste for seasoning, and serve immediately.

Variations: Add some roughly chopped olives and/or finely chopped anchovies.

OUZO, CELERIAC, AND FENNEL REMOULADE

This salad is a wonderful accompaniment to Ouzo and Lemon Cured Salmon (page 38) or Pickled Chicken (page 54). It's also delicious in a sandwich with charcuterie and slices of vine-ripened tomatoes.

Variations: Add 2 tablespoons of capers or some chopped walnuts.

Serves 4–6

1 small celeriac
1 small fennel bulb
Ouzo Mayonnaise (page 43)
2 teaspoons crushed fennel seeds
1 small bunch of finely chopped fresh dill or tarragon
sea salt and freshly ground black pepper
lemon juice, to taste

Cut the ends off the celeriac and peel. Halve it lengthwise and slice into fine juliennes, either by hand or using a mandolin or food processor, or even one of those julienne vegetable peelers! Cut the fennel in half lengthwise and discard the tough outer leaves and core. Separate the layers and thinly slice each one lengthwise to match the celeriac.

Put the celeriac and fennel in a bowl and mix with enough mayonnaise to coat, then stir in the fennel seeds and herbs (and capers or walnuts, if using) and season with sea salt and black pepper; add lemon juice to taste. Cover and refrigerate for at least an hour before serving.

CARROT TABBOULEH

The secret to preparing this beautiful dish lies in the way you chop your herbs—they should be lovingly sliced very finely, to produce thin slivers with minimal bruising. Serve with Carrot Keftedes (page 18).

Serves 4–6

2 medium carrots, peeled and roughly chopped
3 cups fresh flat-leaf parsley, with stems
1½ cups fresh mint leaves, picked
2 tomatoes, finely diced
1 small red onion, finely diced
1 teaspoon ground cinnamon
1 teaspoon ground allspice
juice of 1 lemon
½ cup olive oil
sea salt

Working in batches, put the chopped carrots in a food processor or chopper and pulse-blend until their texture resembles that of bulgur wheat. Pour into a large bowl while you prepare the herbs.

Using a very sharp knife, slice the parsley as thinly as possible, starting at the leafy top and working all the way to the stems. Repeat with the mint leaves and add both herbs to the carrots.

Combine with the tomatoes, onion, and spices. Dress with the lemon juice and olive oil and season with salt before serving.

CARROT SALAD

This is a slightly different, simpler carrot salad that doesn't involve a food processor! Serve with Tahini Sauce (page 160).

1 carrot, peeled and julienned
3 tablespoons raisins, soaked in warm water for 10 minutes
¼ cup almonds (skin on), roughly chopped
½ bunch of fresh flat-leaf parsley, leaves only
2 tablespoons extra-virgin olive oil
1 teaspoon ground cumin
juice of 1 lemon
sea salt

Mix all of the ingredients together, season with salt, and serve.

THE ANATOMY OF A "VILLAGE" (GREEK) SALAD

Since it's one of the most famous and unpretentious dishes that's known worldwide, and one of the most common representations of Greek cuisine, I thought I had to mention the Greek salad. To Greeks it goes by the name of "Horiatiki Salata"— Village Salad.

Although it's a pretty simple affair, opinions are strong about what deviations are acceptable; for me it's a salad that I actually like to serve without any twists (considering the rest of this book that's quite unusual for me!).

A Greek salad should be a balanced blend of bold authentic flavors achieved by using the finest-quality ingredients that become the heart and soul of this healthy and refreshing dish. It's a salad that makes you smile and transports you back to warm climates and sun-drenched beaches!

Serves 4 generously

4 large vine ripe tomatoes provide sweetness and acidity, cut into thick wedges

1 Greek/Lebanese cucumber or ¼ of an English (Greek/Lebanese cucumbers are about 1¼in in diameter) provides freshness and crunch—cut into ½in thick rounds if using Greek or Lebanese, or halve lengthwise and cut into ½in slices if using English

1 red onion provides a bit of bite and "punch," peeled and thinly sliced

16 Kalamata olives and 1½ cups feta provide saltiness

a pinch of dried Greek oregano adds aroma and slight spice

a glug of extra-virgin olive oil provides a creamy richness

a dash of red wine vinegar (optional)

sea salt

Combine the tomatoes, cucumber, red onion, and olives together in a serving bowl and sprinkle with a little sea salt. Place the feta on top, sprinkle with the oregano, and drizzle with olive oil and vinegar, if using; serve immediately with crusty bread to *papara* (dunk) into all the delicious juices that gather at the bottom of the bowl.

"Deviations" include: Purslane leaves, sliced green bell pepper, capers, sliced fennel, parsley leaves.

DINO'S PICKLED CAPER LEAVES

This is a Cypriot delicacy that Greeks can't get enough of! My dad (that's him in the photo) will spend weeks preserving huge jars of caper leaves to serve in his restaurant throughout the summer months. Much less salty than capers (the unopened buds), these tangy leaves are mellower and slightly more citrusy in flavor. Often eaten on their own drizzled with olive oil as part of a mezze, they can also add an exceptionally delicious complexity to dishes. I like to serve them with Fava Purée (page 137) and Wild Fennel and Halloumi Stuffed Rabbit (page 94), Whole Baked Snapper (page 74), Slow-Braised Pork Belly (page 125), or tossed through pasta dishes. Add to a martini for a fun alternative to an olive!

I do appreciate that unless you live in a warm climate where caper bushes grow, it's unlikely you'll pickle these leaves. But I think they're rather special and wanted to share the recipe with you so at least if you see them pickled while on vacation you might now be tempted to try them!

The thorny caper bushes grow almost anywhere in the Mediterranean region and can survive in particularly nutrient-poor soil, although you'll have to hunt the young stems down quickly before the rest of the Greeks do! The stems are a purplish brown with round green leaves the size of a penny.

To pickle the caper leaves, cut about two pounds of short branches from the caper bush, wash well, and cut away any sharp thorns—the smaller ones can stay as they'll soften once pickled. Don't be tempted to taste them, they are really unpleasant—full of mustard oil—which is why they need soaking.

Wash well, place in a large bowl or bucket, cover with cold water, and put a plate on top to keep them submerged. Let soak for five days, changing the water every two days. During this time the leaves will slightly change color and begin to release an unpleasant odor, so don't be alarmed!

Drain the shoots and place in sterilized jars (see page 54). You can either cover with a brine solution made up of 2 tablespoons of sea salt to every 1¾ cups water or a vinegared solution made up of two-thirds water to one-third vinegar (i.e. 2½ cups water, 1¼ cups white vinegar), 1 tablespoon of lemon juice, and 2½ tablespoons of sea salt. Bring the ingredients to a boil, cool, and pour over the soaked leaves to cover.

Seal the jars and let marinate at room temperature for at least a week before using; the longer you leave them, the tastier the leaves will be!

I prefer to pickle mine in a vinegared solution and leave them for a couple of months before using. Refrigerate once opened. Serve drained and drizzled with extra virgin olive oil with one of the suggested dishes.

ALMOND CRUMBS

Use for sprinkling over Pickled Squab (page 52). Equally delicious sprinkled over Zucchini and Caper Linguine (page 67), or over any savory dish to add a little extra texture. See the variations below.

Makes 10½oz

¾ cup whole, skin-on almonds
7oz stale crusty bread (about 5 slices), torn into small pieces
a good glug of olive oil
sea salt
2 teaspoons fresh thyme leaves

Preheat the oven to 350°F.

Spread out the almonds on a baking sheet and roast for 5 minutes. Remove from the heat and let cool.

Put the bread on a separate baking sheet and drizzle with a generous glug of olive oil and a sprinkling of sea salt. Mix with the thyme and place in the oven for 10–15 minutes or until golden and almost crisp. Remove from the oven and let cool.

Put the almonds and bread in a blender and pulse-blend to form crumbs. Season with a little more salt if necessary. Store in an airtight container until required.

Variations: Try adding a few red pepper flakes or fennel seeds, or both, before roasting. Or add a different dimension by including some grated Kefalotyri or Parmesan; this cheesy version is delicious sprinkled over a bowl of hot spaghetti drizzled with chile oil, and is also great with broccoli!

PICKLED VEGETABLES

The Greeks often eat pickled vegetables during Sarokostiani, the 40 fasting days of Lent. They're also a great accompaniment to Ouzo and Lemon Cured Salmon (page 38) as part of a small plate selection, with Lamb Kebabs (page 100) or alongside some White Bean, Artichoke, and Basil Hummus (page 136). This is a great way to preserve the season's best produce. Use any vegetable combination that you like: fennel, turnips, and green beans work really well.

Makes 1-quart jar

1 small carrot, cut diagonally into ¼in-thick slices
1½ cups white cabbage, cut into 2½ x 1¼in pieces
1 small zucchini, cut diagonally into ¼in-thick slices
1½ cups cauliflower, cut into small florets
2 celery ribs with leaves, cut diagonally into ½in lengths
2 cups white wine vinegar
½ cup honey
1 teaspoon fennel seeds
1 cinnamon stick
1 teaspoon allspice berries
1 teaspoon black peppercorns
¾ cup water
extra-virgin olive oil to seal, about ⅔ cup

You will need a warm 1-quart sterilized jar (see page 54).

Blanch all the vegetables in a large saucepan of salted water for 30 seconds. Refresh in ice-cold water, drain well, and pack into the warm sterilized jar.

Heat the vinegar, honey, spices, and water in a saucepan and bring to a boil. Simmer for 2 minutes, then pour over the vegetables. Seal the surface with a little oil—covering any exposed vegetables. Seal and leave in a cool place for at least two days or, better, up to a week before using. Once opened, refrigerate and eat within six weeks. Serve at room temperature.

Variations: To vary the flavor, infuse the vinegar beforehand. Try red chile, citrus zest, bay leaf, fresh oregano, or thyme sprigs; or, for an ancient Greek twist: a little mastic, cardamom pods, cilantro, and cloves.

GRILLED PICKLED EGGPLANTS

This recipe is a great way of using an abundance of eggplants if you're lucky enough to have them growing in your garden! These eggplants are delicious served with Sumac Flatbreads (page 159), Pulled Lamb Burgers (page 106), or marinated olives, feta, and hummus. Grilling the eggplants after they've been brined gives an extra depth of flavor and one I prefer.

Makes 1-quart jar

2 cups white wine vinegar
½ cup honey
2 tablespoons sea salt
½ cup water
2 eggplants, trimmed and cut into ¼in slices
¾ cup sunflower oil, plus extra for drizzling
8 oregano sprigs, picked, or 2 tablespoons dried oregano
4 garlic cloves, finely sliced
1 red chile, finely sliced
¾ cup extra-virgin olive oil

You will need a warm 1-quart sterilized jar (see page 54).

Heat the vinegar, honey, salt, and water in a saucepan and bring to a boil. Put half the eggplants in the pan. Cook until just tender (place a plate on the top to keep them from bobbing around). Remove with a slotted spoon and drain on a baking sheet lined with a cloth. Repeat with the remaining eggplants, then discard the vinegared water.

Preheat a grill pan, drizzle the eggplant slices with a little sunflower oil, and cook, in batches, for 1–2 minutes on each side. Put some of the slices in the bottom of the sterilized jar and sprinkle with a little oregano, garlic, and chile. Repeat the layering, ending with a layer of eggplants.

Warm the oils together over low heat and pour over the eggplants to cover, heating a little more oil if needed; gently tap the jar as you add the oil to release any air pockets. Seal and set aside to cool before refrigerating for at least two days before using. Store in the fridge for up to a month. The eggplants are best brought up to room temperature before serving.

STUFFED AND PICKLED BABY EGGPLANTS

Or Melitzanaki Toursi as they're known in Greece! Delicious with grilled halloumi or Sumac Flatbread (page 159). Make this a week before using.

Makes 1-quart jar

1lb 2oz baby eggplants
1¼ cups white wine vinegar
½ cup honey
1 red chile, finely chopped
2 teaspoons coriander seeds
1 tablespoon sea salt
1 small cinnamon stick
2 tablespoons finely chopped fresh flat-leaf parsley
2 tablespoons finely chopped fresh mint
1 tablespoon finely chopped fresh cilantro
3 garlic cloves, finely chopped
2 tablespoons finely chopped onion
1 carrot, grated
⅓ cup walnuts, chopped
freshly ground black pepper
2 celery ribs
½ cup extra-virgin olive oil

You will need a warm 1-quart sterilized jar (see page 54).

Wash the eggplants, trim the stems, and cook in a saucepan of boiling salted water until just tender, about 5 minutes. Refresh in ice-cold water and drain well.

Heat the vinegar, honey, chile, coriander, salt, cinnamon stick, and ¾ cup water in another pan. Bring to a boil then reduce the heat to a simmer.

Meanwhile, combine the herbs, garlic, onion, carrot, and walnuts in a bowl and season with a little black pepper. Make a lengthwise slit in each eggplant and stuff each with about 1 tablespoonful of the herb mixture. Using a peeler, peel the celery into strips and use to tie the eggplants closed. Pack into the sterilized jar, cover with the hot infused vinegar, and top with olive oil, adding a little more if needed to cover the eggplants. Seal and set aside to cool. Refrigerate for a week before serving at room temperature. They will keep for up to 2 weeks in the fridge, submerged in the pickling liquid.

SESAME BUNS

Try these topped with sun-ripened tomatoes, fresh basil, and a drizzle of olive oil and sea salt. I have also used them with the Pulled Lamb Burgers (page 106) and Fava bean and Mint Hummus (page 132). If you prefer to make a loaf, you'll need to extend the cooking time by about 10 minutes.

Variations: Add 2½ tablespoons chopped Kalamata olives or ¾ cup crumbled feta cheese. You may want to try sprinkling with a little dried oregano, mint, or sumac or anise, cumin, or fennel seeds. Alternatively add a little finely grated lemon zest.

Makes 8 rolls—perhaps more than you'll need, but who can resist freshly baked bread?!

¼oz active dried yeast
2 teaspoons superfine sugar
½ cup warm water
¾ cup warm milk
4 cups all-purpose flour, plus extra for dusting
1 tablespoon butter, diced
1 teaspoon ground allspice
2 teaspoon ground cinnamon
2 teaspoons salt
olive oil, for greasing
1 free-range egg, beaten
sesame seeds, for sprinkling

Mix the yeast, sugar, water, and milk together until the yeast dissolves and let ferment for about 10 minutes.

Sift the flour into a large mixing bowl and rub in the butter until it resembles bread crumbs. Combine with the allspice, cinnamon, and salt (or flavoring of choice). Make a well in the center and pour in the yeast mix. Combine all the ingredients together to form a sticky dough. Turn onto a lightly floured surface and knead until it becomes smooth and elastic, about 20 minutes. This is good for the biceps—alternatively, use the dough hook attachment of an electric mixer. (If you want to add some olives or cheese, now's the time to add and knead them in.) Put the dough in a lightly oiled bowl, cover, and leave in a warm place until doubled in size, about 1–1½ hours.

Turn the dough onto the floured work surface again, punch down to knock out the air, then divide it into 8 pieces and shape them into balls. Use the palm of your hand or a rolling pin to flatten a little. Place on a lightly oiled baking sheet, cover, and set aside to rise for another hour in a warm place until doubled in size. Meanwhile, preheat the oven to 425°F.

Brush the rolls with egg, sprinkle with sesame seeds, and bake for about 10 minutes until they are golden and sound hollow when their bottoms are tapped. Cool slightly on a wire rack and serve warm.

SUMAC FLATBREADS

Flatbreads are quick and easy to prepare. I was in a dilemma over whether to include a pita bread recipe instead, but decided to go with something less traditional. Use to roll around Eggplant Souvlaki (page 68) or Lamb Kebabs (page 100).

Variations: Omit the sumac and flavor with another spice or herb of your choice. Cinnamon or a little ground anise work well, as do oregano and dill. Vary the flavoring to match the dishes you're serving with the flatbreads.

Makes 8 large flatbreads or 12 smaller ones

¾ tablespoon active dried yeast
½ tablespoon superfine sugar
1 cup lukewarm water
3¼ cups all-purpose flour, plus extra for dusting
2 tablespoons sumac, plus extra for sprinkling
3 teaspoons sea salt
1 tablespoon olive oil, for greasing

Mix the yeast, sugar, and water together until the yeast dissolves. Leave in a warm place to ferment for about 10 minutes.

Sift the flour into a large mixing bowl and add the sumac and salt. Make a well in the center and pour in the yeast mix and oil. Combine by hand or with the end of a wooden spoon until the dough comes together. (If you have an electric mixer, use the dough hook.) Once the dough comes together, turn onto a lightly floured surface and knead for about 10 minutes until smooth and elastic. (A little oil on your hands will keep the dough from sticking.) Put the dough in an oiled bowl, cover, and leave in a warm place until doubled in size, about 1–1½ hours.

Turn the dough onto the floured surface, punch down to knock out the air, and divide into 8 balls. Using a rolling pin, roll out each piece into ¼in-thick rounds. Arrange on a baking sheet lined with parchment paper.

Preheat a grill pan, brush each flatbread with a little oil, and cook for about 2 minutes or until golden and puffed on each side. Remove from the heat and sprinkle with sumac. Serve hot.

You can make the dough in advance and keep it in the fridge for two days. If you cook the flatbread in advance, gently reheat in a warm oven before serving.

BAKED GREEN
BEAN SNACK

TAHINI SAUCES

Who doesn't love snacks?! Here's a healthy, tasty one that you can adapt to your heart's content.

Serves 4

1¾ cups green beans
¾ cup bread crumbs
3½ teaspoons garlic powder
3½ teaspoons dried oregano
pinch of dried red pepper flakes/cayenne pepper
finely grated zest of 1 lemon
2 teaspoons salt
freshly ground black pepper
3 egg whites

Preheat the oven to 400°F.

Trim the beans. Mix the bread crumbs in a shallow bowl with the garlic powder, oregano, chile, lemon zest, salt, and a good grinding of black pepper.

Beat the egg whites in a large bowl until frothy, add a quarter of the beans, and mix to coat with your left hand. With the same hand, transfer the beans to the bread crumbs. Using your right hand, toss the beans in the bread crumbs to coat.

Spread out the beans evenly on a nonstick baking sheet lined with parchment paper. Repeat with the remaining beans. Put in the oven. Cook for about 20 minutes until the beans are golden and crisp. I like to serve them in paper cones with a dip such as hummus, tzatziki, or dill yogurt with a wedge of lemon.

Variations: There are many spices and herbs you could use here: substitute the oregano with mint, use orange zest instead of lemon. You could use Greek bread for the crumbs or add some sesame seeds or even a little grated cheese to the mixture. You could also replace the beans with asparagus spears when in season. If you prefer, the beans could also be deep-fried.

Serve with Greek-spiced Chicken Livers (page 60) or as an accompaniment to broiled or barbecued meats or fish. I like to serve the tahini yogurt sauce with blanched or roasted broccoli topped with toasted pine nuts.

SIMPLE TAHINI SAUCE

1 small garlic clove
1 teaspoon sea salt
¼ cup tahini paste
juice of ½ lemon

Crush the garlic with the salt until puréed and transfer to a bowl. Add the tahini and lemon juice and mix well, then whisk in 7 tablespoons water. Cover and refrigerate until ready to serve.

TAHINI YOGURT SAUCE

For a richer tahini sauce, add some Greek yogurt.

1 small garlic clove
1 teaspoon sea salt
¼ cup tahini paste
juice of ½ lemon
a pinch of ground cumin
½ cup Greek yogurt

Crush the garlic with the salt until puréed and transfer to a bowl. Add the tahini, lemon juice, cumin, and 2 tablespoons of water, whisk together, then add the yogurt. If the sauce is too thick, add a little more water. Cover and refrigerate until ready to serve.

DRESSINGS

All these dressings are really simple with ratios for quantities. Simply whisk together, season, and use at once.

LEMON AND OLIVE OIL DRESSING

2 parts extra-virgin olive oil to 1 part freshly
squeezed lemon juice.

The Greeks call this Ladolemono and it's the standard dressing for flavoring salad, grilled fish, and cooked vegetables. If you want to embellish the dressing, add a little chopped herb, such as flat-leaf parsley, dill, mint, or cilantro.

OIL AND VINEGAR DRESSING

2 parts extra-virgin olive oil to 1 part red or white
wine vinegar, plus a pinch of dried oregano

You can extend the flavor by whisking with a teaspoon of Dijon mustard, or adding some chopped herbs, as above. Or, add everything along with some chopped capers, shallots, and olives. For another twist, add some chopped salted anchovy fillets, using a little of their oil in the dressing. For a touch of sweetness, add a little honey to the base recipe.

OUZO LEMON DRESSING

3 parts olive oil to 2 parts lemon juice to 1 part ouzo
to ¼ part white wine vinegar

Use this to dress green salads, such as the Horta Salad on page 145, chilled watermelon and feta salad, or even roasted rabbit.

OUZO RED WINE VINEGAR DRESSING

2 parts olive oil to 2 parts red wine vinegar to 1 part
ouzo, plus a few drops of honey

You can add any herb of your choice and a little finely chopped shallot. A great dressing with chilled watermelon and crumbled feta.

LEMON OREGANO SALT

There are so many uses for this delicious flavored salt. You can use it to season tomatoes or mozzarella, fresh peas, asparagus, or borlotti beans; or, of course, potatoes, whether roasted, mashed, or sliced. Try adding it to pasta dough or to freshly made popcorn, along with a drizzle of olive oil and lemon juice. It is also fabulous sprinkled onto fish or meat before cooking, or into olive oil for bread-dipping. It even works in margaritas…

1 lemon
¼ cup sea salt
1 teaspoon dried oregano (Greek of course!)

Finely grate the lemon zest and put in a mortar (I find that this is best done with a microplane). Add the salt and pound with the pestle until combined. Then simply mix in the oregano and you're ready to rock.

If not using the salt immediately, sprinkle the salt over a baking sheet lined with parchment paper and let dry a little before storing in an airtight container in a cool place.

Variations: You could use orange or lime zest instead of lemon and dried mint in place of oregano. Clementine zest makes a wonderful salt, blended with crisp slices of Serrano ham—great sprinkled over fish and popcorn.

MARINATED OLIVES

Try serving these olives mixed with cubed feta for an added twist. Another lovely way to serve your olives is to toast them in a grill pan to warm through and lightly char, then mix with one of the marinades below and serve warm with crusty bread, halloumi, and feta. It's up to you whether you choose pitted olives or not. Rinse the olives of any brine they may come in before marinating.

ORANGE AND OREGANO MARINATED OLIVES

1/3 cup extra-virgin olive oil
2 garlic cloves, thinly sliced
zest of 1 orange, stripped with a vegetable peeler, excess pith removed
4 oregano sprigs, picked
1 thyme sprig, picked
10½oz black and/or green Kalamata olives
2 tablespoons red wine vinegar

Heat the oil in a small saucepan, add the garlic, orange zest, oregano, and thyme, and cook over low heat for 2 minutes to infuse. Add the olives and cook for another 2 minutes. Pour into a non-reactive container, add the vinegar, and let marinate for 10 hours. The longer you wait, the better they'll be!

Variations: Replace the oregano and thyme with the finely chopped leaves from a rosemary sprig. For some extra pep, add a chopped red chile. Warm a tablespoon of lightly crushed coriander seeds in olive oil and add. Finish the olives with some freshly chopped parsley or parsley and mint. Or use tangerine/clementine zest instead.

LEMON AND CILANTRO MARINATED OLIVES

1 tablespoon coriander seeds
1/3 cup extra-virgin olive oil
zest (stripped with a vegetable peeler, excess pith removed) and juice of 1 lemon
10½oz green Kalamata olives
a handful of cilantro leaves, roughly chopped, to serve

Lightly crush the coriander seeds and put in a small saucepan with the olive oil and lemon zest. Cook gently over low heat to infuse. Add the olives and warm for 2 minutes. Pour into a non-reactive container, squeeze in the juice from the lemon, and stir. Let marinate overnight, stirring through the fresh cilantro before serving.

FENNEL, CHILE, AND LEMON MARINATED OLIVES

1 tablespoon fennel seeds
1/3 cup extra-virgin olive oil
2 garlic cloves, finely sliced
1 red chile, seeded and diced
4 strips of lemon zest, removed with vegetable peeler, excess pith removed
10½oz green Kalamata olives

Dry-fry the fennel seeds in a small saucepan, then add the oil, garlic, chile, and lemon zest and warm through. Add the olives, transfer to a non-reactive container, and let marinate for as long as possible. Add a squeeze of lemon juice too, if you'd like.

^{4/}SWEET PLATES

ANISE AND SESAME CRACKERS

Try these crackers with some Greek yogurt drizzled with mountain honey and slices of blood oranges for a fabulous breakfast. They are also great with a soft blue cheese or as a base for the Rabbit Rillettes on page 58, topped with fresh figs and honey. You can vary the flavors by sprinkling with finely chopped fresh rosemary for a more savory version, or ground cinnamon for a sweeter one. I sometimes scatter the crackers with sliced almonds instead of sesame seeds.

Makes 20–30 crackers

zest of 1 lemon, stripped with a vegetable peeler,
  excess pith removed
½ cup extra-virgin olive oil
3¼ cups all-purpose flour, sifted, plus extra for dusting
¾ teaspoon baking powder
1 tablespoon sea salt
1 tablespoon anise seeds
1 tablespoon superfine sugar
1 cup milk
¼ cup ouzo or pastis

To finish:
superfine sugar
honey
5 tablespoons sesame seeds

Put the lemon zest in a small saucepan with the olive oil. Gently warm through until the oil is tepid. Turn off the heat and let infuse. (You could use store-bought lemon oil instead, if you prefer.)

Sift together the flour and baking powder in a bowl and mix in the salt, anise seeds, and sugar. Make a well in the center and add the milk, ouzo, and ¼ cup of the lemon-infused olive oil. Stir to combine, then turn onto a lightly floured work surface and knead lightly to form a moist, smooth dough. Wrap in plastic wrap and rest for 25 minutes. You can leave the dough in the fridge for a day if preparing ahead.

Preheat the oven to 425°F and line several baking sheets with parchment paper.

Divide the dough into walnut-sized pieces and roll each lengthwise on a lightly floured surface as thinly as possible—I like to roll them into long strips, but you could make them round if you prefer. Place on the baking sheets, prick with a fork, then brush with some of the lemon oil and scatter with sugar. Bake in batches until golden and crisp, about 10 minutes.

As soon as they come out of the oven, drizzle the crackers with honey and scatter with sesame seeds. Cool on a wire rack. They will keep for up to 5 days in an airtight container. If they lose their crispness, refresh them for a few minutes in a hot oven.

RHUBARB, ROSE, AND ALMOND GRANOLA

Greeks really aren't big on breakfast. They generally just have a coffee (usually black) and a "rusk"—a dry biscuit that's very hard to swallow unless it's dunked! It's not the most exciting of breakfasts, so I've come up with a Greek-inspired granola and added some rhubarb for that delicious color! You will need to start making the granola 24 hours in advance to allow the oats to soak.

Variations: I quite like to serve the granola topped with a mix of almonds, roasted pumpkin, sunflower and sesame seeds, prepared by drizzling with olive oil, sprinkling with sugar and a pinch of cinnamon, and roasting until golden.

Serves 4

7oz rhubarb, cut into 1½in pieces
3 tablespoons honey, plus extra for serving
½ cup freshly squeezed orange juice
2 tablespoons rose water*
3 cups rolled oats
1 teaspoon ground cinnamon
⅔ cup Greek yogurt
½ cup (shelled weight) toasted almond slices or pistachios, shelled and chopped if you prefer

* If using rose extract instead, adjust the amount as it's much more concentrated—up to 2 teaspoons, but taste as you go; you can always add more, but you can't take away.

Put the rhubarb in a large saucepan with the honey and orange juice and poach gently over low heat for approximately 10 minutes until the rhubarb has just softened. Cool and drain the cooking liquid into a glass jug and add the rose water (or extract).

Mix the cooking liquid with the oats, cinnamon, yogurt, half the almonds or pistachios, and half the rhubarb. Stir to combine and refrigerate overnight, allowing the oats to soak.

Serve the granola topped with the remaining poached rhubarb, almonds or pistachios, and a drizzle of honey.

BANANA, OAT, AND ALMOND SMOOTHIE

This is a nutritious smoothie for any time of the day, but is a particularly great way to start one! I like to use dates to sweeten my smoothie but you could use honey instead. It's also great for using up overripe bananas (store these in the freezer until you're ready to use).

Variations: Try adding a pinch of cinnamon or vary the fruit; ripe peaches, oats, and honey make a delicious alternative.

Serves 1 (or 2 if you feel like sharing!)

1 banana, torn into small pieces
1 Medjool date, finely chopped, or
   1 tablespoon honey, to taste
1 tablespoon whole, skin-on almonds
¼ cup oats
½ cup Greek yogurt
½ cup cold milk

Put all the ingredients in a blender and process until smooth. Pour into a glass and serve immediately. Add some ice when blending to make it extra cold.

GREEK COFFEE

Coffee culture is an essential part of Greek life; it's a beverage of community and conversation. It provides a morning wake up, mediates a mid-morning chat, refreshes you after a siesta, and is the fuel that gets you through the night's eating, drinking, and discussion. Being invited in for coffee with the villagers is considered a form of acceptance; it's a crucial part of social conduct and hospitality.

Coffee rules:

– **The coffee must be sipped, slowly, to allow the grains to settle.**

– **The coffee shop is considered a "man's domain" and it is not the done thing for women to go there, especially alone. It's the place men go to discuss politics, chat, play backgammon and cards, and, of course, smoke a cigarette! Women have their coffee at home or at a pâtisserie.**

– **Coffee making is regarded as "women's work"! (These aren't my rules, by the way!)**

– **Coffee is always served with a glass of chilled water.**

– **Greek coffee is Greek coffee, not Turkish coffee!**

– **Coffee is always ordered by the name that signifies its sweetness:**

Skettos (bitter and without sugar)

Metrios (medium-sweet)

Glykis (sweet)

Briki is the name given to the long-handled lipped coffee pot in which coffee is prepared and it comes in a variety of sizes. Traditionally made from brass, its shape allows the heat to be distributed slowly and evenly as the coffee is brought to a boil.

The art of coffee making:

To make one cup of metrios coffee, measure one (espresso-sized) coffee cup of water and pour into the briki, add one heaping teaspoon of "Greek" very finely ground coffee, and one teaspoon of sugar and stir over low heat until the coffee and sugar dissolve. As soon as the coffee starts to froth, watch over it until the coffee almost rises to the top, then immediately take off the heat. Never serve a coffee that's boiled over—it's the equivalent of serving poison! Remove from the heat and leave for a second or two before pouring into the cup. If you're making coffee for more than one person be sure to divide the "kaimaki" (froth) evenly between each cup, followed by the coffee. Allow the coffee time to settle for a minute before drinking. (They say whoever has the most "kaimaki" on their coffee is the "luckier" and for any bubble, that's a kiss!)

Serve with a glass of cold water and a spoon sweet (see page 52) if you're entertaining! In my dad's taverna they heat the coffee in embers, an age-old tradition. Some people like to flavor their coffee with a little mastic that's been ground with a little sugar and add to the coffee as it comes off the heat.

In the 18th century it was customary for "a young man" seeking a girl's hand in marriage to be served a cup of coffee by her family. If the coffee was served sweet the parents approved, if served bitter, the man would politely leave, thank them, and never be seen again.

There is a saying that you can't hide anything from the mocha; the maker's mood is reflected in the resulting cup.

Coffee readings!

Fortune-telling is also considered a woman's job!

After the coffee's drunk, the sediment is slowly swirled around the cup, which is then turned upside down onto the saucer where it's left for awhile to sit. The "kafetzou" (the woman who can read the grains) turns the cup over, studies the grains, and then predicts your future!

GREEK COFFEE ON A PLATE

Because of its social significance and the deep, rich flavor that I love, I decided to devote several recipes to coffee as an ingredient in the form of dessert, playing on the different textures and sweetnesses. Serve these recipes as individual desserts or plan ahead and make all 6 in miniature form to serve as part of a Greek coffee tasting dessert—Greek Coffee on a Plate. You'll need to plan carefully, but I promise you the result will be mindblowing!

CHOCOLATE SOIL

A chocolate-scented soil for garnishing Greek Coffee on a Plate or for sprinkling over ice cream.

Makes enough for 8

⅓ cup unsweetened cocoa powder
¾ cup all-purpose flour
3 tablespoons superfine sugar
a pinch of salt
7 tablespoons unsalted butter, diced

Preheat the oven to 300°F.

Sift the dry ingredients through a coarse strainer into a bowl. Add the butter and mix to combine. Spread over a silicone mat or baking sheet lined with parchment paper and bake until dry, about 15–25 minutes. Cool, then crumble. Store in an airtight container until required.

GOAT'S MILK AND GREEK COFFEE PANNA COTTA

Panna cottas are one of my all-time favorite desserts, the secret of a good one being in the "wobble"! It should be just gently set. The goat's milk adds a light touch and the coffee delicately flavors like a latte. Serve as part of the Greek Coffee on a Plate by making miniature versions, serving 2–3 per person. Or make larger as individual portions, accompanying them with Anise and Sesame Crackers (page 166). Ask your local coffee shop for some disposable expresso cups to set your panna cottas in—they work fabulously well and also save on washing up! Once set, pierce the bottom of each cup with the point of a knife and dip in a little hot water before turning out. The piercing will make turning the panna cottas out a whole lot easier. If I'm making miniature ones I use 2 tablespoon plastic salad dressing cups—you should get in good with your local deli or start saving them up. Alternatively, set the mix in several shallow containers and spoon onto the plate.

Serves 6 or 8 as a tasting plate
(makes 18 x 1oz mini portions or 6 x 2½oz portions)

1 cup goat's milk
1 cup heavy cream
½ vanilla bean, seeds scraped out
2 heaping tablespoons good-quality instant
  coffee granules
⅓ cup superfine sugar
2½ gelatin sheets (about ⅛oz in weight)

Pour the goat's milk and cream into a saucepan, add the vanilla, coffee, and sugar, place over low heat, and bring just to a boil, then remove from the heat.

Meanwhile, soak the gelatin in cold water until softened, about 5 minutes (check the package though as some are "quick soaking"). Squeeze the water from the leaves and add them to the hot cream, stirring to dissolve. Pass through a fine strainer into a bowl. Pour into molds and cool completely before refrigerating until set, about 3½ –4 hours, depending on the size.

To serve, dip the molds briefly in hot water and gently turn onto a plate.

GREEK COFFEE CHOCOLATE GANACHE

This is a deep, dark and velvety smooth ganache, intensely flavored with coffee and not a drop of cream in sight. "Like coffee for chocolate!" Serve as part of Greek Coffee on a Plate or with coffee-poached pears, plums, or apples.

Serves 4 or 8 as a tasting plate

7oz dark chocolate, 70 percent cocoa solids
6 heaping teaspoons Greek coffee*
¾ cup water

*If you don't have Greek coffee, make up ⅔ cup of strong instant coffee—make sure it's almost boiling when adding to the chocolate.

Bash the hell out of the chocolate while it's still in its package "Jamie Oliver style," by whacking it a few times on the work surface! Then place the chocolate in a heatproof bowl.

Mix the Greek coffee and water in a small pan over low heat and heat until the coffee froths—once it starts to rise, take off the heat immediately. Pour into a bowl and let settle, then carefully ladle or pour out the coffee, measuring ⅔ cup. (I've tried passing the coffee through a strainer before, but the grains are way too fine and I've ended up with a gritty ganache!) Pour the measured coffee into a saucepan and gently reheat over low heat until just boiling. Pour in the chocolate to melt and whisk until smooth.

Cool and let set. Refrigerate until required, removing from the fridge 1 hour before serving for maximum flavor and texture. Serve teaspoonfuls of the ganache as part of the Greek Coffee on a Plate.

Variation: You can add extra flavor to the ganache with a pinch of one of the following spices: ground cardamom, ground cloves, ground cinnamon, or ground anise. You could also add a little freshly grated lemon or orange zest.

GREEK COFFEE AND CARDAMOM JELLY

Cardamom is most often used in sweet Greek pastries, its heavenly scent and aromatic spicy sweetness adding a wonderful depth of flavor. Cardamom was introduced to the Greeks through the Egyptians via India. It was in Cairo that I first tasted an Egyptian coffee scented with cardamom, and I've loved it ever since.

The jelly is an extension of the coffee, lightly set with agar-agar. Serve it as part of the Greek Coffee on a Plate or on its own with some Condensed Milk Ice Cream (page 183) or a little whipped cream flavored with a pinch of cinnamon.

Serves 4 or 8 as a tasting plate

1 cup strong Greek coffee* or ¼ cup good-
  quality instant coffee granules
⅓ cup superfine sugar
8 cardamom pods, lightly crushed
1 small cinnamon stick
2 cloves
¾ teaspoon agar-agar

*If using Greek coffee, use 8 heaping teaspoons of coffee and 1¾ cups of water, follow the method on page 171, and let settle before pouring the coffee from the grains. Measure 1 cup and proceed.

Put the coffee in a saucepan, add the sugar, cardamom, cinnamon, and cloves and heat gently until almost to a boil, then discard the cinnamon stick. Whisk in the agar-agar and continue to whisk over medium–high heat for 2 minutes. Pass through a strainer into a shallow container or into individual molds and let cool and set before refrigerating for 2 hours before serving.

GREEK COFFEE "FRAPPÉ" GRANITA

I love the smooth texture of the sweet condensed milk with the robust textured iced coffee crystals. This is my take on a frappé. Serve as part of the Greek Coffee on a Plate or on its own as an easy yet quirky dessert.

Serves 4 or 8 as a tasting plate

½ cup superfine sugar
2⅓ cups hot strong Greek coffee*
½ x 14oz can sweetened condensed milk

*Use 16 heaping teaspoons of coffee and 2½ cups of water, follow the method on page 171, and let settle before pouring the coffee from the grains. Measure 2⅓ cups and proceed.

Stir the sugar into the hot coffee until it completely dissolves and set aside to cool. Meanwhile, place a shallow baking sheet big enough to contain the coffee in the freezer. Once the coffee is cold, pour it into the baking sheet.

Freeze until half frozen (about 2–2½ hours), then stir with a fork and freeze for another 1–2 hours until just frozen. Stir once more with a fork, breaking the mixture into small, even-sized ice crystals. Once ready to serve, remove the baking sheet from the freezer and leave for 20 minutes before breaking into small ice crystals with a fork as above.

Pour the condensed milk into the bottom of each glass or bowl and top with granita. Serve immediately.

Variation: You can add depth of flavor by infusing the coffee with some crushed cardamom pods (I'd add about 10)—let them infuse while the coffee cools then pass through a strainer. Spooning some softly whipped cream over the top at the end is naughty but nice!

COFFEE CUSTARD DOUGHNUTS WITH FENNEL SEED SUGAR

Traditional Greek doughnuts, "loukoumades," are soaked in a sweet syrup after frying and make me feel the need to have my dentist on speed dial. These lighter alternatives can be made mini-size and served as part of Greek Coffee on a Plate. Custard, you say? Yes, it's nostalgic—use crème pâtissière if you prefer (see the recipe on page 199 and replace the pistachio paste with 2 teaspoons of instant coffee). Thanks to Lucas for his guidance on my doughnuts!

Makes 46 mini doughnuts or 14 large

3 tablespoons unsalted butter, diced
2 cups all-purpose flour
1 heaping tablespoon fast-action yeast
2 tablespoons superfine sugar
a pinch of salt
½ cup milk
½ cup cream
vegetable oil for deep-frying—about 1 quart

For the coffee custard (makes 2 cups):
¼ cup superfine sugar
2 tablespoons good-quality instant coffee granules
3 tablespoons cornstarch
1 cup milk
1 cup heavy cream

For the fennel seed sugar:
1 cup superfine sugar
5 tablespoons fennel seeds, lightly toasted

In a large bowl, rub the butter into the flour using your fingertips until incorporated. Add the yeast, sugar, and a pinch of salt and make a well in the center. Gently warm the milk and cream to body temperature (98°F), pour into the flour and, using your fingertips or the end of a wooden spoon, mix until incorporated. Turn onto a lightly floured surface, grease your hands with a little oil, and knead until soft and smooth. Place in a lightly greased bowl, cover with a cloth, and let rise in a warm place until doubled in size (about 40 minutes).

Transfer the dough to a lightly floured surface and knock back. Roll it into balls – about ¾-inch diameter for mini doughnuts, or 1¼-inch diameter for large. Cut the parchment into squares big enough to hold 4 mini doughnuts or 2 large, allowing room for rising. Dust the paper with a little flour and place the doughnuts on top. Place on a baking sheet and cover with a cloth. Let rise in a warm place for about 30 minutes or until well risen.

While the doughnuts rise, make the custard and fennel sugar.

For the custard, combine the sugar, coffee, and cornstarch together in a small bowl and mix with a little of the cold milk to make a smooth paste. Heat the remaining milk and cream in a saucepan almost to a boil. Reduce the heat to low. While whisking, pour the custard mixture into the hot milk. Continue whisking over low heat until the custard thickens. Transfer to a bowl and cover with a layer of plastic wrap to prevent a skin from forming. Once cooled, transfer to a piping bag (if filling the doughnuts—if you prefer, you can serve the custard on the side).

For the fennel sugar, combine the sugar and fennel seeds in a spice grinder, food processor, or pestle and mortar and blend to a fine powder. Place on a shallow baking sheet.

To cook the doughnuts, heat the oil in a deep-fryer or large saucepan to 175°F (which means that a cube of bread will brown in 30 seconds). Lower the doughnuts in batches of two into the oil, paper included. (This keeps you from having to lift the doughnuts up, which will knock the air from them, resulting in a lighter doughnut.) Remove the paper with tongs within seconds of adding to the oil, and fry the doughnuts until crisp and golden, turning frequently. Drain using a strainer and roll immediately in the fennel seed sugar.

Cut the doughnuts down the center and fill with custard using the piping bag. Alternatively, serve with a bowl of warm custard on the side to "dunk."

Variations: Add ½ cup of raisins pre-soaked in Commandaria/Mavrodaphne/port to the dough when mixing. Fennel seeds are my favorite flavor but you could vary the sugar by replacing the fennel with some finely grated orange or lemon zest. For a summery alternative fill the doughnuts with lemon curd flavored with a little ouzo and roll in lemon sugar mixed with chopped basil. Alternatively, replace the coffee custard with chocolate ganache.

COMMANDARIA, CHOCOLATE, AND FIG TRIFLE

Commandaria is a sweet dessert wine made in the foothills of the Troodos mountains in Cyprus. Mavron and Xinisteri grapes are harvested late and left to dry in the sun to concentrate their sugar content. The wine is then left to mature in oak barrels for at least two years, resulting in a deliciously honey sweet, spiced, deep and tannic aromatic wine. Its history dates back to the Crusaders, taking its name from an Order of the Knights of the Cross. Look out for the St. John variety, whose knights made the wine famous throughout the Kingdoms of Europe. Greece's equivalent is Mavrodaphne, made in Patras in the Peloponnese, so you can use that instead, or substitute with port if unavailable.

Every good trifle needs custard and good old Bird's is the one for me—you'll have to trust me on this one! You can find it in speciality stores or online.

You'll need to start this recipe in the morning of the evening you are serving. If you'd prefer a lighter trifle, top with a little crème fraîche as opposed to the cream.

Serves 6–8

For the chocolate and Commandaria filling:
2 cups Commandaria
¾ cup superfine sugar
10½oz dark chocolate (70 percent cocoa solids), broken into small pieces
2 gelatin sheets

For the custard:
⅓ cup Bird's custard powder
¼ cup superfine sugar
1 cup milk
1 cup heavy cream
1 vanilla bean, split and seeds scraped out

16 lady fingers
cocoa powder, for dusting

For the caramelized figs:
8 figs, halved
¼ cup brown or superfine sugar

For the cream:
¾ cup heavy cream
¼ cup confectioners' sugar
¾ cup Greek yogurt

For the filling, combine 1¼ cups of the Commandaria and the sugar in a saucepan and bring to a boil over medium heat. Add the chocolate, remove from the heat, and stir until smooth. Soak the gelatin in cold water for 5 minutes, then squeeze of any excess water, add to the chocolate mixture, and stir to dissolve. Let cool a little before refrigerating until almost, but not fully, set.

Next, mix the custard powder and sugar with a little of the milk to form a smooth paste. Heat the cream, remaining milk, and vanilla seeds in a saucepan until almost to a boil. Reduce the heat and slowly whisk in the custard mixture, whisking until the custard thickens. Remove from the heat and cover the surface with plastic wrap to keep a skin from forming; let cool.

Break the lady fingers into small pieces and divide between six or eight individual glasses or place in a single bowl, depending on how you're serving the trifle. Drizzle the pieces with the remaining Commandaria and top evenly with the slightly cooled custard.

For the figs, preheat a large frying pan. Toss the figs in the sugar, add to the pan, and sear over medium heat for 2 minutes or until just softened and caramelized. Spoon the figs over the custard and put in the fridge until the filling is almost set. Then spoon the filling evenly over the figs and return to the fridge until fully set.

For the cream, whisk the cream and confectioners' sugar in a bowl to form soft peaks. Fold through the yogurt, then spoon over the filling and refrigerate for 20 minutes. Serve the trifle chilled, dusted with a little cocoa.

Variations: You could also scatter with nuts, such as roasted hazelnuts, almonds, or walnuts. And use dried or fresh cherries instead of the figs (if using dried, pre-soak in a little Commandaria).

METAXA FRUIT AND CHOCOLATE MOUSSE

Little servings of chocolate bliss!

Greece's legendary brandy adds luxury and depth to this decadent dessert that's quick and easy to prepare. Serve in espresso cups, mini jars, or ceramic ramekins.

Serves 6–8, depending on gluttony

7oz dark chocolate (70 percent cocoa solids), broken into small pieces
1¼ cups heavy cream
⅔ cup Metaxa
3 free-range egg yolks
¼ cup superfine sugar
¼ cup raisins
4 dried figs, cut into small pieces

To serve:
½ cup whipped cream
12 Amaretti cookies, coarsely crushed
ground cinnamon, for dusting

Put the chocolate, cream, and half the Metaxa in a heatproof bowl placed over a pan of simmering water, making sure the bowl doesn't come into direct contact with the water. Stir occasionally until melted and smooth. Remove the bowl from the heat and let cool.

Put the egg yolks and sugar in a separate heatproof bowl and whisk over simmering water (again avoiding contact with the water) until thick and pale, about 5 minutes. Remove from the heat and stand the bowl on a cloth (to keep the bowl in one place!) and slowly whisk in the cooled melted chocolate until combined. Divide the mixture between your chosen container and refrigerate for 1 hour or until set.

Heat the remaining Metaxa with 3 tablespoons water and pour over the raisins and figs. Soak until plump, about 10 minutes.

To serve, top the desserts with the soaked fruit, along with some whipped cream, crushed Amaretti cookies, and a sprinkling of cinnamon.

Variations: You could try topping the chocolate desserts with cherry or orange spoon sweets and a sprinkling of nuts to add texture. Instead of Amaretti, you can use some roasted crushed almonds, hazelnuts, or walnuts, or a combination of all three. If Metaxa's not your thing, try soaking the raisins in Commandaria (see left).

TAHINI CHOCOLATE CAKES WITH CRÈME FRAÎCHE

More chocolate bliss! Hot chocolate cakes oozing with fudge-like gooey centers. Intensely flavored with an added tahini twist. Serve with crème fraîche or Sesame Peanut Brittle Ice Cream (page 182).

The number of cakes you make will depend on the size of your mold—you can use dariole molds or even ovenproof tea cups. I used ½-cup molds and made six.

Makes 4–6

1 stick + 2 tablespoons unsalted butter, plus extra for greasing
⅓ cup cocoa powder, plus extra for dusting
3 tablespoons sesame seeds
5½oz dark chocolate (70 percent cocoa solids), broken into pieces
3 free-range eggs
1 cup superfine sugar
5 tablespoons tahini
½ cup all-purpose flour
a pinch of salt

To serve:
zest of 1 lime
crème fraîche or ice cream

Preheat the oven to 350°F.

Grease your molds with butter and dust them with cocoa powder. Sprinkle the bottom of each with sesame seeds.

Melt the chocolate and butter in a heatproof bowl over a pan of simmering water, but make sure that the bowl doesn't actually touch the water. Stir until melted and smooth, then remove from the heat and let cool a little.

Whisk the eggs and sugar in a large bowl for a good 5 minutes, until pale and fluffy. Add the tahini and stir until combined, then gradually whisk in the cooled chocolate. Sift the flour, cocoa powder, and salt into the chocolate mixture and fold in. Pour the mixture into the molds and place on a baking sheet.

Cook the cakes for 12–14 minutes. They should be a little soggy so a skewer inserted will not come out clean, but you'll have a lovely fudge-like center! Depending on the size of your molds, you may need to cook them for a little less, or a little longer.

Cool a little before gently turning onto a plate. Dust with a little more cocoa powder and grate a little lime zest over the top. Serve with crème fraîche or ice cream.

The mixture can be made ahead of time and stored in the fridge for two days, although you'll need to allow a few minutes' more cooking time if cooking from cold.

SESAME AND PEANUT BRITTLE ICE CREAM

I always remember my Dad bringing home a bag of sweets as a special treat for me and my sister. It was full of chocolate bars (he could never just buy two!), Fry's Turkish Delight (which my sister loved; I just used to nibble the chocolate around the edges), and these nut brittle rings. Made of caramelized peanuts and sesame seeds, they were so sweet and very tough on your teeth—a dentist's nightmare! This recipe is an ice cream version of those childhood memories— soft sesame ice cream with salty-sweet peanut brittle. You need to start the ice cream the day before to allow the flavors to infuse.

Serves 4–6

¾ cup sesame seeds (2 tablespoons will be for the brittle)
2 cups milk
3 tablespoons tahini
1 cup heavy cream
⅔ cup superfine sugar
6 free-range egg yolks

For the peanut brittle:
⅔ cup superfine sugar
¾ cup salted peanuts
2 tablespoons reserved roasted sesame seeds

Preheat the oven to 350°F.

Sprinkle the sesame seeds on a baking sheet and roast for about 5 minutes, until golden. Pour all but 2 tablespoons into a saucepan and add the milk and tahini. Stir over low heat until almost boiling, then turn off the heat and let infuse for a couple of hours or overnight in the fridge.

Pour the sesame-infused milk through a fine strainer into a clean saucepan. Add the cream and bring to a boil. While it is heating, whisk together the sugar and egg yolks in a large bowl until pale and thick.

Pour the milk over the egg yolk mixture, whisking all the time, then return to the pan and stir continuously with a wooden spoon over low heat until the mixture thickens and coats the back of the spoon (technically, that'll be about 180–185°F). Strain into a large bowl placed over iced water then, once cool, freeze in an ice-cream machine following the manufacturer's instructions.

Meanwhile, make the peanut brittle. Put the sugar in a small saucepan over low heat. Don't be tempted to keep stirring—leave it to caramelize. Once it's dark golden and shiny, remove from the heat and mix in the peanuts and reserved sesame seeds. Quickly pour onto a lightly oiled baking sheet and let cool.

Break the brittle into coarse pieces and bash into smaller ones with the bottom of a saucepan (it's best to put the brittle between two sheets of parchment paper to do this). Alternatively, pulse-blend in a food processor until coarsely ground. Stir through the sesame ice cream, reserving a little to sprinkle over the top for garnish.

CONDENSED MILK ICE CREAM

One of my favorite desserts as a kid was condensed milk and canned peaches! There's something incredibly comforting about the stuff; it's the secret "naughty but nice" ingredient in an iced coffee and I've even seen the unsweetened version used in a white sauce in Cyprus! Elevate condensed milk to new heights with this ice cream. Serve with Greek Coffee Frappé Granita (page 175) for the ultimate frappé, or with roasted peaches and Anise and Sesame Crackers (page 166).

Serves 4–6

⅔ cup milk
1 cup heavy cream
4 free-range egg yolks
¾ cup sweetened condensed milk
a pinch of salt

Pour the milk and half the cream into a saucepan and bring to a boil. Put the egg yolks in a bowl and, while whisking, slowly pour the hot cream mixture over them. Return the mixture to the pan and gently cook over medium heat, stirring continuously, until the mixture thickens and coats the back of the spoon.

Pass through a strainer into a bowl and stir in the remaining cream, condensed milk, and a pinch of salt. Let cool before churning in an ice-cream machine, following the manufacturer's instructions.

If you don't own an ice-cream machine, try this simple version: whisk 1¼ cups heavy cream and 1 teaspoon of vanilla extract to soft peaks, then whisk in the condensed milk and a pinch of salt. Spoon into a plastic container, cover, and freeze until firm, beating at hourly intervals with a whisk to break up the ice crystals that form. Remove from the freezer 5 minutes before serving.

Variations: Flavor the ice cream with some ground cardamom or a little orange water or saffron, and top with crushed pistachios.

CINNAMON, WALNUT, AND GREEK YOGURT ICE CREAM

A quick, easy, and very adaptable ice cream. See my extensive list of variations below!

Serves 4–8

¾ cup heavy whipping cream
½ cup light brown sugar, packed
2 teaspoons ground cinnamon
1 teaspoon vanilla essence
2 cups Greek yogurt
1¼ cups roasted chopped walnuts

Put the cream, sugar and cinnamon in a small saucepan and warm gently, stirring to dissolve the sugar. Remove from heat, add the remaining ingredients, and stir to combine. Cool and refrigerate before pouring into a pre-chilled ice-cream machine and churn according to manufacturer's instructions.

Variations: Once the ice cream has churned, swirl through a little homemade apple/pear sauce or fig/date purée. (To make apple/pear sauce, peel, core, and chop 2 apples/pears and cook in a little butter over low heat until softened; purée until smooth. I don't add any sugar to the sauce as I think the ice cream is sweet enough.) Or blend the ice-cream base, minus the nuts, with a banana and freeze as above, adding the walnuts while churning so as to keep the texture. Try adding a little finely grated orange rind to the ice-cream mixture to freshen, or substitute the walnuts for almonds or hazelnuts.

ORANGE AND FENNEL SEED ICE CREAM

The flavor of anise features quite heavily in Greek cuisine. Here I've used fennel seeds, which have a light anise/licorice flavor and balance perfectly with the zesty orange. The ice cream is delicious served with my Chocolate, Orange, and Anise Tart (page 186). 0

Serves 4–6 as a dessert, or 12 as an accompaniment to the Chocolate, Orange, and Anise Tart

1¾ cups heavy cream
zest of 2 oranges
2 teaspoons ground fennel seeds
6 free-range egg yolks
¾ cup superfine sugar
1 cup whole milk

Heat the cream, orange zest, and fennel seeds in a saucepan until almost boiling. Turn off the heat and let infuse for a minimum of 30 minutes.

Whisk together the egg yolks and sugar in a large bowl until pale and thick. Reheat the infused cream, adding the milk over medium heat until almost boiling. Slowly whisk the cream into the egg mixture until combined.

Return the mixture to the pan and stir continuously over low heat with a wooden spoon until the mixture is thick enough to coat the back of the spoon.

Strain into a bowl placed over a pan filled with ice and stir occasionally until cool. Churn in an ice-cream machine following the manufacturer's instructions.

BLACKBERRY AND OUZO SORBET

Blackberries grow wild throughout the Troodos mountains in Cyprus. They're notably smaller than the ones in the US, but their flavor is just as sweet. I've always thought blackberries have a natural affinity with licorice and anise flavors so thought this sorbet would make a refreshing palate cleanser or dessert. Serve with a swirl of Greek yogurt to add an extra texture dimension or alongside the Chocolate, Orange, and Anise tart (page 186).

Serves 4

½ cup superfine sugar
1 cup water
1lb blackberries, washed and hulled
1 tablespoon lemon juice
¼ cup ouzo

Put the sugar in a small saucepan with the water and place over low heat, stirring until the sugar dissolves. Remove from heat and set aside to cool.

Purée the blackberries with lemon juice in a blender until smooth and then pass through a fine strainer into a bowl, discarding the seeds. Mix together with the cooled sugar syrup and ouzo and chill before churning in an ice-cream machine following the manufacturers' instructions.

Alternatively, put the mixture in a small saucepan/baking dish (it will freeze faster in a metal pan) and freeze, whisking every few hours with a fork to break down the ice crystals that form. Continue to do so until the sorbet is frozen.

You can also place the sorbet in a food processor to break up the ice crystals, but you'll need to return it to the freezer again to freeze so it's firm enough to serve.

However you freeze it, for best results remove from the freezer 10 minutes before serving as the sorbet will have a much better texture.

CHOCOLATE, ORANGE, AND ANISE TART

This smooth and gooey chocolate tart, set in a crisp, almond crust, is rich with dark undertones of coffee and spiked with anise. It is delicious with Orange and Fennel Seed Ice Cream (page 185).

You will need a 10in, ¾in deep, fluted, nonstick tart pan with a removable bottom.

Serves 12

For the crust:
2 cups all-purpose flour, plus extra for dusting
¼ cup almond flour
¾ teaspoon ground allspice
grated zest of 1 orange
10 tablespoons cold butter, diced
½ cup confectioners' sugar
a pinch of salt
1 free-range egg, plus 1 egg yolk
flour, for dusting

For the filling:
1 cup heavy cream
5 star anise, processed to a powder, or 3 teaspoons ground anise
finely grated zest of 1 orange
10oz dark chocolate (70 percent cocoa solids), broken into small pieces
6 free-range egg yolks

Process the flour, almond flour, allspice, orange zest, butter, sugar, and a pinch of salt in a food processor until they resemble bread crumbs. Add the egg and extra yolk and pulse-blend until the dough comes together. Remove and knead lightly on a floured surface, then roll into a ball, wrap in plastic wrap, and chill in the fridge for an hour.

Roll the dough between two sheets of parchment paper until it's large enough to line the tart pan. Prick the dough with a fork and refrigerate for 20 minutes. Preheat the oven to 350°F.

Line the crust with parchment paper and baking beans, place on a baking sheet, and bake blind for 15–20 minutes, until lightly colored. Remove the beans and paper and bake for another 5 minutes or until dry and golden. Set aside.

Put the cream, anise, orange zest, and chocolate in a heatproof bowl over a pan of barely simmering water and heat gently, stirring occasionally, until the chocolate has melted—make sure the bowl doesn't make contact with the water. Set aside to cool a little.

Whisk the yolks into the chocolate mixture one at a time, then pour the mixture into the crust and cook for 5–8 minutes or until just set—give the baking sheet a gentle shake to test. Carefully remove from the oven and let cool before refrigerating. Remove from the fridge 40 minutes before serving.

WATERMELON AND GREEK BASIL ICE POPS

If you don't own any ice pop/ popsicle molds, you can freeze these in silicone muffin or ice trays, or even paper espresso cups, and skewer with bamboo sticks. Great for dinner parties or used as the "ice" in a vodka-based cocktail (now we're talking!).

Variations: Try using half watermelon juice, half strawberry juice for a refreshing variation; mint in place of basil also works well.

Serves 6–8

½ cup superfine sugar
½ cup water
a handful of fresh basil leaves
1lb 10oz watermelon flesh, seeded and diced
1 tablespoon lime juice
Greek basil leaves, to garnish (optional)

Put the sugar and water in a small saucepan over medium heat until the sugar dissolves, then remove from the heat. Add the basil leaves, stir to combine, then cover with plastic wrap and let infuse and cool.

Meanwhile, place the diced watermelon and lime juice in a blender and process until smooth. Pass through a fine strainer into a bowl. You should end up with around 2½ cups watermelon juice.

Once the basil-infused syrup is cool, pass through a strainer into the watermelon juice and mix well. If you've got some Greek basil, stir some leaves through the mixture. Pour into ice pop molds and freeze, remembering to add sticks halfway through if your molds come without!

STRAWBERRY, ROSE, AND BASIL RICE PUDDING

Traditionally, Greek rice pudding is flavored with cinnamon and vanilla. Sometimes it's even finished with egg yolks, making it extra rich and creamy—my version's a lot lighter. Use half almond milk to add an extra flavor. The tops of the strawberries, which would otherwise be discarded, can be used to make a wonderful syrup that can be used in this recipe or folded through Greek yogurt or poured over ice cream.

Serves 4

½ cup short-grain rice
5 cups milk, or 2½ cups milk and 2½ cups unsweetened almond milk
1 vanilla bean, split and seeds scraped, or a few drops of essence
4½oz strawberries
½ cup water
3 tablespoons superfine sugar, plus an extra 1½ tablespoons for the syrup
a few drops of rose extract or up to 1 tablespoon rose water, to taste (see note on page 194)
Greek basil leaves, to serve (optional)

Place the rice in a strainer and rinse under cold running water for 1 minute. Put in a saucepan with the milk and vanilla seeds and bring to a boil, then reduce the heat to low. Simmer the rice, stirring occasionally, until tender— about 35–40 minutes.

Meanwhile, prepare the strawberries and syrup. Cut the tops from the strawberries and place the tops in a small saucepan with the water and 1½ tablespoons sugar. Cook over very low heat for 20–30 minutes or until the mixture is syrupy and the strawberry tops have bled. Strain the syrup, discarding the tops. Cut the strawberries into eighths and set aside.

Once the rice is soft, stir in the rest of the sugar and mix to dissolve before removing from the heat. Stir in the rose water or extract to taste. Add a few drops at a time—you can always add more but can't take it out.

Serve the rice pudding warm topped with the strawberries, syrup, and torn basil leaves, or serve chilled if you prefer. I like to sprinkle a little freshly milled black pepper on top of mine; try it, you will be pleasantly surprised by the taste. You could also top with a few toasted almond flakes.

Variations: Try flavoring the pudding with a little orange flower water instead of the rose water and top with some Poached Apricots (page 197). Or replace the rose water with a little almond extract and top with cherries or peaches.

WATERMELON MAHALEPI

This is the only way I eat mahalepi, flavored with one of my favorite fruits, the watermelon. Traditionally, mahalepi is made with water and cornstarch—not the most enticing dessert, even when it's served sprinkled with sugar and rose syrup! I'm in a minority, though, as the Greeks love it.

Variations: You can try various flavors—grape would be interesting, as would orange, scented with fresh basil. Just make a purée of the fruit, pass through a fine strainer, and then make up to the required volume with water.

Serves 4

For the rose syrup:
⅔ **cup water**
1¼ **cups sugar**
2 **tablespoons rose water, or a few drops of rose essence**
juice of ½ lemon
red food coloring

4½lb **watermelon, cut into small pieces (discard the rind)**
½ **cup cornstarch**
⅓ **cup superfine sugar**

To garnish:
glug of rose syrup
8 **strawberries**
around 16 chopped pistachios
rose petals or violas (optional)

To make the syrup, place the water and sugar in a pan and heat until the sugar dissolves. Turn up the heat and boil for 3 minutes, then take off the heat and stir in the rose water and lemon juice and taste for strength. Add a tiny drop of food coloring and pour into a sterilized jar or bottle. Once cooled, seal and refrigerate.

Place the watermelon pieces in a blender and blend until smooth. Pass through a fine strainer into a large jug or bowl. Do this a little at a time as you'll need to push the purée through the strainer with a spoon. You should end up with around 2½ cups watermelon juice in total—make up with a little water if necessary.

Whisk the cornstarch with a little of the juice to make a smooth slurry, then whisk with the remaining juice and pour into a saucepan. Whisk over low heat until the mixture comes to a boil and thickens. Cook for 1 minute. Turn off the heat and whisk in the sugar until it dissolves.

Pour the mixture into four shallow bowls that have been sprinkled with a few drops of cold water—this will make removing the mahalepi a lot easier, as it stops them from sticking. Let cool before refrigerating overnight or for at least 3 hours.

Turn the mahalepi from of their molds (they should easily slide out—add a splash of water if they don't). Serve in deep dishes, topped with a glug of rose syrup and garnished with strawberries, pistachios, and rose petals or violas if you have them.

MILK AND BAY PIE

Known as Galaktoboureko, this is a divine pie consisting of milk and semolina custard encased in crisp filo and soaked in syrup. I've infused the custard with bay and the syrup with orange instead of the traditional lemon. Serve with some poached figs, quinces (see right), or lavender-roasted plums (see Plum and Lavender Baklava recipe on page 200).

Variations: To vary, you can replace a little of the syrup water with some brandy or use lemon zest and juice instead of orange. Alternatively, when in season, use bergamot zest and juice for a refreshing change. You could also try adding a layer of roast nuts to the filo crust before topping with custard for added texture.

Makes 12–15 slices

4 cups milk
2 bay leaves
1 vanilla bean, split and seeds scraped out
2 tablespoons unsalted butter
1¾ cups superfine sugar
1 cup fine semolina
4 free-range eggs
2 sticks unsalted butter, melted
9 sheets of filo dough
ground cinnamon and confectioners' sugar (optional),
   for dusting

For the syrup:
juice of 1 orange
1¼ cups superfine sugar
2 strips of orange zest
1 bay leaf

Preheat the oven to 325°F. Put the milk in a pan with the bay leaves and vanilla bean and seeds and heat almost to a boil. Add the 2 tablespoons butter and two-thirds of the sugar; stir until dissolved. Whisk in the semolina, reduce the heat to medium, and whisk until the custard thickens, about 5 minutes. Remove from the heat and let cool a little. Whisk the eggs and remaining sugar until pale and thick, then whisk into the custard. Cover with a layer of plastic wrap to prevent a skin from forming while you prepare the filo.

Grease the sides and base of an 8 x 13in baking dish with the melted butter. Cut the filo dough in half lengthwise, butter and layer 7 pieces together, and line the bottom and sides of the dish. Spread the custard mixture (discarding the bay leaves and vanilla bean) over the base. Butter and layer all but two of the remaining filo sheets and place on top of the custard. Fold the sides neatly over the filo and top with a double layer of buttered filo. Liberally brush the surface with butter and lightly score the surface, forming about 12–15 diamonds, squares, or rectangles. Bake in the oven for about 50 minutes, until the crust is golden and the custard is set.

For the syrup, add enough water to the orange juice to make 1 cup, put in a saucepan with the remaining ingredients, and bring to a boil. Simmer for 5 minutes then pass through a strainer. Pour over the pie as soon as it comes out of the oven and set aside for 2 hours to cool. Cut into portions and dust with cinnamon and, if you feel like it, a little confectioners' sugar before glazing with a blow torch or under a hot broiler. Serve at room temperature.

POACHED QUINCES

Not only will a bowl of quinces fill the air with a delicate aromatic perfume, they taste great too! They go well with Milk and Bay Pie (see left) or with a dollop of Greek yogurt.

Variations: When quinces are out of season, you could make this with apples or pears, but you will need to adjust the cooking time considerably. Check them regularly after 20 minutes. As with the quinces, the cooking time will depend on the ripeness of the fruit.

Serves 4–8

2 cups water
⅓ cup sugar
2 star anise
1 bay leaf
¼ cup honey
2 cloves
juice of ½ lemon
2 large quinces

Preheat the oven to 350°F.

Place the water in a medium, ovenproof saucepan with the sugar, star anise, bay leaf, honey, cloves, and lemon juice. Bring to a boil, stirring to dissolve the sugar.

Scrub the quinces and cut them in half; leave the seeds and cores attached as they aid the color. Place in the saucepan, cover with parchment paper and foil, and cook in the oven for about 1½ hours, or until the quince are tender but not mushy. Let cool and serve drizzled with their syrup.

ALMOND, ROSE WATER, AND CHOCOLATE MALLOMAR CHIMNEYS

Mallomar chimneys are one of my favorite treats! Making them can take a bit of mastering, though, so this is a simplified version. I've flavored the marshmallow with rose water and used an almond cookie for the base, but there are many variations you could try, including those I've suggested below.

Variations: Omit the rose water and flavor with some ground cinnamon and coffee; or use a little orange flower water or star anise and orange to flavor the marshmallow.

* Rose essence is more highly flavored than rose water, so just a few drops equals the strength of a tablespoon of rose water. Use with care—too much, and you'll end up with a teacake that tastes like moisturizer! Taste as you go— you can always add, but you can't take away.

Makes 16

For the cookie base:
¼ cup superfine sugar
3 tablespoons butter
2 tablespoons milk
1 cup almond flour
¾ cup all-purpose flour, plus extra for dusting
a pinch of salt
1 teaspoon baking powder

For the marshmallow:
3 free-range egg whites
¾ cup superfine sugar
2 tablespoons corn syrup
a pinch of salt
2 tablespoons rose water, or a few drops of rose essence*
18 whole almonds (skin on), finely chopped in a food processor
10½oz dark chocolate, 70 percent cocoa solids, broken into pieces

Start by making the cookie base. Cream the sugar and butter together until pale. Slowly add the milk, and don't panic if it looks like a curdled mess. Sift in the remaining ingredients and stir to form a dough. Wrap in plastic wrap and refrigerate for about 30 minutes to firm up.

Preheat the oven to 325°F.

Put the dough on a lightly floured surface and roll out to about ¼in thick. Cut into rounds measuring about 2¾in in diameter. Place on a baking sheet lined with parchment paper and refrigerate for 10 minutes. (You can chill them overnight, or even freeze them, if preparing in advance.)

Bake the cookies for about 15 minutes, until firm and golden, then cool on a wire rack.

Meanwhile, make the marshmallow. Put all of the ingredients except the almonds and chocolate in a large heatproof bowl set over a pan of simmering water, making sure that the bowl and water don't come into contact. Whisk by hand or with an electric mixer continuously for about 15 minutes, until the mixture has doubled in size and forms stiff peaks. Fold in the chopped almonds and spoon the marshmallow into a piping bag and set aside.

Put the chocolate in a bowl over simmering water, again making sure the bowl and water don't touch, until melted and smooth. Dip one side of each of the cooled cookies into the chocolate and place on a wire rack to set.

Make a small cut in the piping bag and pipe spiral marshmallow "chimneys" about 2½in tall on top of each cookie. Let the teacakes set in a cool place for about 10 minutes and then *nappe* (coat) each with the melted chocolate (you may need to re-melt it a little). Let the chocolate set for around 5–10 minutes before serving—if you can wait that long!

APRICOT AND ORANGE BLOSSOM MERINGUES

I can't tell you how many meringue recipes I've tried throughout my cooking career and the disasters I've had along the way! But thanks to Dan Lepard my meringue nightmares are over. Not only is Dan a lovely man, he's also an exceptional baker and chef. His meringue recipe employs a totally different technique from the usual one: instead of gradually mixing sugar or hot sugar syrup (as in Italian meringue) into the egg white, he dissolves the sugar and whites together over low heat before whisking, resulting in the best meringue I have ever made— with just the right combination of crispness and chewiness. Use your leftover yolks to make the Dried Fig Leaf Pasta (page 116).

Serves 4–8

½ cup free-range egg white (about 4 eggs)
1 cup superfine sugar
a pinch of salt
1 tablespoon white wine vinegar
a handful of toasted sliced almonds
2 tablespoons orange flower water

You will also need a pair of clean disposable latex gloves.

Preheat the oven to 225°F. Line two baking sheets with parchment paper or silicone mats.

Put the egg whites, sugar, salt, and vinegar in a scrupulously clean saucepan or metallic mixing bowl. Place over very low heat and keep the mixture moving with your hand (the gloves stop any oils from being released from your hands) to dissolve the sugar and prevent the whites from cooking. Alternatively, place in a bowl set over a pan of simmering water and stir with your gloved hand until the sugar has dissolved and the mixture is warm to the touch. The aim is to warm the egg and sugar mixture to body temperature (98°F).

Transfer the mixture to the bowl of an electric mixer fitted with a balloon whisk attachment. Whisk on high speed until the meringue is thick, glossy, and holds stiff peaks. It will take about 10–15 minutes to achieve this. Fold in the almonds and orange flower water.

Drop 6 (or 8, if you prefer a smaller dessert) even spoonfuls of meringue onto the prepared pan. Either way, leave a 1½in gap between each. Taking a teaspoon, make a dent in the center of each and swirl up the sides, creating a little carrier for the filling.

Place in the preheated oven and bake for 1¾ hours until the outsides of the meringues are firm and crisp. Let cool.

Once cool, fill with the Orange Blossom Cream (below) and Poached Apricots (right) or filling of your choice. You can store the unfilled meringues in an airtight container for up to three days.

Variations: You can also use rose water, cinnamon, coffee, or saffron to flavor the meringues. Vary the fillings depending on what fruit's in season, or fill with whipped cream, Greek Coffee Chocolate Ganache, and Greek Coffee and Cardamom Jelly (See Greek Coffee section, page 174).

ORANGE BLOSSOM YOGURT CREAM

Serves 4

¾ cup heavy cream
2 tablespoons superfine sugar
2 tablespoons orange flower water
¾ cup Greek yogurt

Place the cream, superfine sugar, and orange flower water in a bowl and whisk to form soft peaks; fold through the yogurt and refrigerate until required. If you prefer a sweeter cream, add a little extra sugar.

POACHED APRICOTS

Sun-kissed apricots eaten fresh from the tree are heavenly and bursting with flavor. But the reality of being in an apricot "orchard" is rare for many of us, and we end up with the mixture of sweet, tart, and sometimes floury apricots found at the store. For that reason, I like to lightly poach them. These apricots are great served with Greek yogurt for breakfast— maybe not if you poach them in wine; but then again it could be a great way to start the day!

The pits can be cracked open to reveal an almond-tasting nut inside that is absolutely delicious and well worth the bother. When I worked at El Bulli many years ago we used these as a garnish, which meant cracking open hundreds of pits; they are harder than an almond shell—say no more! Serve these nuts sprinkled over the apricots.

Serves 4–8

1lb 2oz fresh apricots
⅔ cup superfine sugar
¾ cup water

Cut the apricots in half and remove their pits. Put the apricots in a large saucepan with the sugar and water. Place over low heat and slowly bring to a boil, then remove from the heat and allow the apricots to cool in their cooking liquid. It's really important not to let them overcook as they will lose their shape and you'll end up with apricot soup! Cool and refrigerate until required.

Variations: Alternatively, you can add bay leaf, rosemary, or bergamot or orange zest to add flavor to the apricots. You could replace the water with a dessert wine such as a Sauternes or Muscat, in which case you may want to reduce the sugar a little.

PISTACHIO CREAM CHOUX BUNS WITH CHOCOLATE ORANGE BLOSSOM SAUCE

You'll need to give yourself a little time to make the three elements involved: choux buns, pistachio cream, and orange blossom sauce, but these retro classics will fill you with joy! The choux buns are an adaptable recipe you can use for profiteroles, éclairs, or gougeres (just omit the sugar)

Choux pastry was one of the first things I learned as a pastry apprentice while at The Café Royal, London. In those days it was the trend to make "choux swans," I'm slightly embarrassed about it now!

Makes 12 large buns (or 24 small)

1 cup all-purpose flour
½ cup milk
1 tablespoon sugar
a pinch of salt
5 tablespoons unsalted butter, diced
½ cup cold water
4 eggs, beaten

To finish:
Pistachio Crème Pâtissière or Crème Diplomat, to fill (see opposite)
Chocolate Orange Blossom Sauce (see opposite)

Preheat the oven to 400°F.

Sift the flour onto a sheet of parchment paper and set aside. Put the milk, sugar, salt, butter, and water into a large saucepan over medium heat. As soon as the liquid comes to a boil, remove from heat and add the flour in one shot; then immediately beat vigorously with a wooden spoon to combine.

Return the pan to low heat and continue vigorously beating for a minute or two until the mixture comes together and easily leaves the sides of the pan clean. Transfer the batter to a large bowl, or the bowl of an electric mixer, and let cool for around 4 minutes. You can speed this process up by whisking at a low speed; if you're not lucky enough to have an electric mixer, use a small hand-held one.

When cool, increase the speed and, while still whisking, add the eggs a little at a time, making sure that they are fully incorporated before adding more. You will end up with a lovely shiny, smooth, and thick batter that you can use for profiteroles, choux buns, or éclairs.

Lightly grease a baking sheet and sprinkle with cold water as though blessing it with Holy water. (A French pastry chef taught me this trick, which is similar to placing a bowl of water in the bottom of the oven when baking bread: the water turns to steam in the hot oven and helps the buns to rise.) Pipe or spoon tablespoonfuls of the choux pastry onto the prepared pans and bake until well risen and starting to color, about 10–15 minutes, depending on the size.

Lower the oven to 325°F and bake for another 10–15 minutes until lightly browned and crisp. Remove from the oven and immediately make a small hole in the side of each—this releases the steam caught inside and keeps them from getting soggy. Let cool on a wire rack. Only when they are completely cool should you fill them; you don't want to ruin your efforts and make them soggy again!

If you want to fill your buns with Crème Diplomat, now is the time to whisk the ½ cup heavy cream to ribbon stage and fold into the Pistachio Crème Pâtissière. Cut the choux buns open and fill with the cream, then sandwich back together. Drizzle with Chocolate Orange Blossom Sauce before serving or dust with confectioners' sugar and serve little individual bowls of chocolate sauce on the side.

Variations: If you'd prefer a speedier version, simply fill the choux buns with pistachio ice cream. To add an element of surprise, you can fill the buns with cream and a little chopped orange blossom Turkish delight.

PISTACHIO CRÈME PÂTISSIÈRE

I use pistachio paste for this (which you can buy online). If pistachios aren't your thing, omit the paste and flavor with a little rose or orange blossom water. You could also infuse the milk with coffee beans, although you'd need to allow it to infuse (covered) for a few hours before using—or just add 2 tablespoons of instant coffee to the finished pastry cream.

Makes 1¾ cups

1 vanilla bean, split lengthwise and seeds
  scraped out
1⅔ cups whole milk
3 free-range egg yolks
⅓ cup superfine sugar
¼ cup cornstarch
1oz pistachio paste
½ cup heavy cream, optional (see Crème
  Diplomat, right)

Put the vanilla seeds and the milk in a saucepan and bring milk to a boil over low heat.

Meanwhile, in a large bowl, whisk together the yolks and sugar until pale, then whisk in the cornstarch.

Once the milk has almost boiled, pour about a third over the egg mixture, whisking continuously, then pour this mixture back into the saucepan and return to the heat. Whisk continuously over low heat until the mixture boils and thickens. Unlike crème anglaise, pastry cream should be boiled, enabling the flour to cook out. Remove from the heat and whisk in the pistachio paste.

Place the Crème Pâtissière in a clean bowl to cool, covering the surface directly with plastic wrap (this will prevent a skin from forming). Refrigerate until required and use within two days.

CRÈME DIPLOMAT

You can use the pistachio cream as it is for the choux buns, but I like to fold in some whipped cream to make it lighter. This version is actually known as Crème Diplomat, or Diplomat Cream.

Place the heavy cream in a bowl and whisk to "ribbon stage," when soft peaks are forming. Fold into the cold pistachio cream and refrigerate until required. If you're preparing this ahead of time, don't add the whipped cream to the pistachio cream until the day it's required—it will keep much better this way.

CHOCOLATE ORANGE BLOSSOM SAUCE

¾ cup heavy cream
2 tablespoons butter, diced
½ cup superfine sugar
¾ cup cocoa powder
2oz dark chocolate (70 percent cocoa solids),
  broken into small pieces
¾ cup water
2 teaspoons orange flower water

Place all the ingredients except the water and orange flower water in a saucepan. Add the plain water and bring to a simmer over low heat, whisking continuously until the sauce thickens. Remove from the heat and flavor with orange flower water. I've suggested 2 teaspoons, but you may find you need a touch more, depending on the brand. The flavor is meant to be subtle.

PLUM AND LAVENDER BAKLAVA

Not everyone would associate plums with Greek cuisine, although prunes and plum brandy are fairly big exports.

While in Cyprus, I saw an abundance of plum trees lining the mountainous roadside, along with lavender, which inspired me to put the two together. The succulent, tart plums cut through the sweetness of the baklava, and the lavender brings a touch of elegance with its delicate perfume, taking this traditional dessert on a flavor adventure.

Serve with some Greek yogurt, crème fraîche, or Condensed Milk Ice Cream (page 183).

Makes 20 pieces

For the syrup:
¾ cup honey
1¼ cups lavender sugar, or 1¼ cups superfine sugar plus 2 tablespoons dried lavender
1 cup water
1 cinnamon stick
2 strips of orange rind

For the baklava:
11 red plums, halved, pitted, and cut into thirds
½ cup lavender sugar, or ½ cup superfine sugar plus 1 tablespoon dried lavender
3 cups roasted almonds, finely chopped
1½ cups roasted hazelnuts, finely chopped
1 stick + 2 tablespoons unsalted butter, melted
16 sheets (or 8 large sheets) of filo dough

Put all the syrup ingredients in a saucepan and bring to a boil, then simmer for about 5 minutes until the syrup begins to thicken. Set aside to cool, discarding the cinnamon stick and orange rind.

Preheat the oven to 400°F.

Toss the plum slices with half of the lavender sugar and put in a roasting pan. Cover with foil and roast for 20 minutes, then remove the foil and let cool. Strain off any cooking juices and reserve.

Reduce the oven temperature to 350°F. Mix the nuts with the remaining lavender sugar and set aside.

Brush the bottom of a 10 x 12in baking pan with melted butter. If using large sheets of filo, cut in half lengthwise. Brush one layer with butter and top with another; repeat until you have a 6 layer buttered filo "sandwich." Sprinkle a third of the nut mixture evenly over the filo, followed by a third of the sliced plums.

Take another 6 layers of filo, brush each with butter as before, and lay on top of the nuts and plums. Scatter the filo dough with more nuts and plums and repeat as above. To finish, brush the remaining four layers of filo with butter and place on the top. Using a sharp knife, score a diamond pattern on the surface, no deeper than the top layer of nuts. Brush with melted butter and sprinkle with a few drops of water to prevent the filo from curling during cooking.

Bake for 35–40 minutes, or until golden. Remove from the oven and pour the cold syrup over the baklava and set aside to cool for a few hours, or overnight, until the syrup has been fully absorbed. Add the reserved plum cooking juices to the syrup or reserve to fold through Greek yogurt. Serve at room temperature.

APPLE AND GREEK YOGURT CAKE WITH METAXA BRANDY SYRUP

A step up from poundcake and a cup of coffee! Sweet apples, earthy walnuts, and a generous soaking of brandy syrup take this cake to new heights. Serve with a large spoonful of crème fraîche or Greek yogurt for an afternoon snack—or, in fact, at any time of day.

Variations: You can use ¾ cup apple juice for the syrup instead of the water and brandy, but make sure you reduce the sugar to ⅔ cup.

Serves 8–10

For the cake:
1 stick + 1 tablespoon unsalted butter, plus extra for greasing
1½ cups self-rising flour, plus extra for flouring
1 cup superfine sugar
5 free-range eggs
1 cup Greek yogurt
1 teaspoon baking powder
2 teaspoons ground cinnamon
3 apples, peeled, cored, and diced into ½in pieces

For the syrup:
⅔ cup water
¾ cup superfine sugar
¼ cup honey
⅓ cup Greek brandy (Metaxa)

To serve:
½ cup toasted walnuts
Greek yogurt or crème fraîche

Preheat the oven to 350°F. Grease and flour an 8in springform pan.

Whisk together the butter and sugar in a large bowl until pale. Gradually beat in the eggs until combined, then stir in the yogurt. Sift in the baking powder, cinnamon, and flour, mix until combined, then add the diced apple. Pour the batter into the prepared pan and bake for about 1 hour or until a skewer inserted into the center comes out clean. Remove from the oven and let cool in the pan while you make the syrup.

Combine the syrup ingredients in a small saucepan, bring to a boil, and simmer until the liquid has thickened to a syrup.

Pierce the surface of the cake with a skewer and pour the syrup over the top, leaving a little to toss the walnuts in. Let the syrup soak into the cake for about 10 minutes, then sprinkle with walnuts tossed in syrup and serve with Greek yogurt or crème fraîche.

INDEX

Acknowledgments

Heart-filled thanks to the following super talented and creative people who've been a part of this book:

Kyle Cathie, for your support and continued faith in me; can't believe this is book three!

Sophie Allen, for guiding my vision into a reality with humor and encouragement along the way.

Tabitha Hawkins, what a joy! You so nailed my translation of rambling thoughts with such perfect props and ideas; your attention to detail is second to none. You're a ray of sunshine.

Linda Tubby, for bringing my recipes to life with such perfection and beauty—much respect!

Jenny Zarins, you have captured everything I ever dreamt of and more with your simply stunning photography: from the breathtaking beauty of the Troodos and its people to my food, bringing life and soul to the pages of this book with such amazing energy and warmth. ("Too much!"). I feel humbled to have worked with you.

Georgie Clarke—not to be forgotten, one of the most organized people I know; it's been a pleasure.

Buro Creative—JJ and Roly—thank you all for translating my vision into such a beautifully designed book. It's everything I could ever wish for and more!

Tara O'Sullivan, thank you for your endless edits and for picking up all the loose ends and bringing everything together with so much dedication—much appreciated.

Emily Hatchwell and Stephanie Evans, for copyediting and proofreading—I wouldn't want your job!

You've all done me so unbelievably proud and I feel blessed to have worked with such a talented team. Together you've simply "Smashed it"!

More thanks to:

Elena, "the real Greek," for tirelessly testing my recipes and generously sharing your knowledge and your endless support; you're a true gem!

Allison, you're the best friend anyone could ever have. Thanks for your relentless support and encouragement, and recipe testing, too!

To the rest of my friends, thanks all for the support and encouragement. I'm sorry for my unsociable behavior while writing this book.

To Muna for divine inspiration re: the title and to Katy—you're a star!

Thank you also to the people of Gerakis for welcoming me into their homes and generously sharing their knowledge and skills with me; to Odysea for their generous contribution of produce while shooting the book, and to Nikki and Monica for organizing.

Dad, I hope this book does you and my Greek heritage proud.

Mom, always remember Luuttcaatsitw!

Xx